# NATEF Correlated Task Sheets

*for*

# Automotive Fuel and Emissions Control Systems

## Fourth Edition

## James D. Halderman

**PEARSON**

Boston  Columbus  Indianapolis  New York  San Francisco  Hoboken
Amsterdam  Cape Town  Dubai  London  Madrid  Milan  Munich  Paris  Montreal  Toronto
Delhi  Mexico City  Sao Paulo  Sydney  Hong Kong  Seoul  Singapore  Taipei  Tokyo

**Editorial Director:** Andrew Gilfillan
**Program Manager:** Holly Shufeldt
**Project Manager:** Rex Davidson
**Editorial Assistant:** Nancy Kesterson
**Team Lead Project Manager:** JoEllen Gohr
**Team Lead Program Manager:** Laura Weaver
**Director of Marketing:** David Gesell
**Senior Marketing Assistant:** Les Roberts
**Procurement Specialist:** Deidra M. Skahill

**Media Project Manager:** Noelle Chun
**Media Project Coordinator:** April Cleland
**Cover Designer:** Integra Software Services, Ltd.
**Creative Director:** Andrea Nix
**Art Director:** Diane Y. Ernsberger
**Full-Service Project Management and Composition:** Integra Software Services, Ltd.
**Printer/Binder:** Edwards Brothers Malloy
**Cover Printer:** Edwards Brothers Malloy

**PEARSON**

10 9 8 7 6 5 4 3 2 1

ISBN-10:    0-13-379981-6
ISBN-13: 978-0-13-379981-1

# Table of Contents

**Chapter 20**    **Fuel-Injection Components and Operation**

**Chapter 21**    **Gasoline Direct-Injection Systems**

**Chapter 22**    **Electronic Throttle Control System**

**Chapter 23**    **Fuel-Injection System Diagnosis and Service**

# Fire Extinguisher

**Meets NATEF Task:** None Specified

Name _____ Date _____ Time on Task _____

Make/Model _____ Year _____ Evaluation: 4  3  2  1

_____ **1.** Describe the location of the fire extinguishers in your building or shop and note the last inspection dates.

| Type of Extinguisher | Location | Inspection Date |
|---|---|---|
| _____ | _____ | _____ |
| _____ | _____ | _____ |
| _____ | _____ | _____ |
| _____ | _____ | _____ |

_____ **2.** Do any of the fire extinguishers need to be charged?

_____ Yes (which ones) _____

_____ No

_____ **3.** Where can the fire extinguishers be recharged? List the name and telephone number of the company.

_____  _____

_____ **4.** What is the cost to recharge the fire extinguishers?

a. Water = _____

b. $CO_2$ = _____

c. Dry chemical = _____

# Vehicle Hoisting

**Meets NATEF Task:** Safety requirement for engine performance  (A8).

Name _____     Date _____     Time on Task _____

Make/Model _____     Year _____     Evaluation:  4  3  2  1

### Getting Ready to Hoist the Vehicle

_____  **1.** Drive the vehicle into position to be hoisted (lifted) being certain to center the vehicle in the stall.

_____  **2.** Pull the vehicle forward until the front tire rests on the tire pad (if equipped).

_____  **3.** Place the gear selector into the park position (if the vehicle has an automatic transmission/transaxle) or in neutral (if the vehicle has a manual transmission/transaxle) and firmly apply the parking brake.

_____  **4.** Lower the driver's side window before exiting the vehicle. (This step helps prevent keys from being accidentally being locked in the vehicle.)

_____  **5.** Position the arms and hoist pads under the frame or pinch-weld seams of the body.

### Hoisting the Vehicle

_____  **6.** Slowly raise the vehicle about one foot (30 cm) off the ground and check the stability of the vehicle by attempting to move the vehicle on the lift.

_____  **7.** If the vehicle is stable and all pads are properly positioned under the vehicle, continue hoisting the vehicle to the height needed.

> **NOTE:** Best working conditions are at chest or elbow level.

_____  **8.** Be sure the safety latches have engaged before working under the vehicle.

### Lowering the Vehicle

_____  **9.** To lower the vehicle, raise the hoist slightly, then release the safety latches.

_____  **10.** Lower the vehicle using the proper operating and safety release levers.

> **CAUTION:** Do not look away while lowering the vehicle. One side of the vehicle could become stuck or something (or someone) could get under the vehicle.

_____  **11.** After lowering the hoist arms all the way to the floor, move the arms so that they will not be hit when the vehicle is driven out of the stall.

We Support
NATEF

# Safety Check

**Meets NATEF Task:** Safety requirement for engine performance (A8).

Name _____ Date _____ Time on Task _____

Make/Model _____ Year _____ Evaluation: 4  3  2  1

_____ 1. Check the headlights (brights and dim).

_____ 2. Check the taillights.

_____ 3. Check the side marker lights.

_____ 4. Check the license plate light.

_____ 5. Check the brake lights.

_____ 6. Check the turn signals.

_____ 7. Check the back-up lights with the ignition switch "on" (engine "off") and the gear selector in reverse.

_____ 8. Check the windshield wipers (all speeds) and wiper blades.

_____ 9. Check the heater-defroster fan (all speeds).

_____ 10. Check the condition of the tires (must have at least 2/32" of tread) and the tire pressure. Do not forget to check the spare tire!

_____ 11. Check for looseness in the steering wheel (less than 2" of play).

_____ 12. Check the 4-way emergency flashers.

_____ 13. Check the horn.

_____ 14. Listen for exhaust system leaks.

_____ 15. Check the parking brake (maximum 8-10 "clicks" and should "hold" in drive).

# Work Order

**Meets NATEF Task:** (A8-A-1) Complete work order. (P-1)

Name _____ Date _____ Time on Task _____

Make/Model _____ Year _____ Evaluation: 4 3 2 1

Fill in the customer and vehicle information, plus the customer concerns and related service history.

---

UAS Automotive
1415 Any Street
City, State 99999

**NATEF**
ASE CERTIFIED PROGRAM

---

**Customer Information**      Name _____
Daytime _____      Address _____
Evening _____      City _____ State _____ Zip _____

**Vehicle Information**
Year _____      Model _____
Color _____      Mileage _____
VIN _____

---

**Materials**
_____
_____
_____
_____
_____
_____
_____
_____
_____
_____
_____
_____
_____
_____
_____
_____

**Customer Concern** _____
_____
_____
_____
_____
_____

**Related Service History** _____
_____
_____
_____

**Labor Performed**
_____
_____
_____

**Root Cause of Problem** _____
_____
_____

**Totals**

| Materials | _____ |
| Labor | _____ |
| Misc. | _____ |
| Sub Total | _____ |
| Tax | _____ |
| TOTAL | _____ |

**Customer Authorization**

X _____

# Vehicle Service Information

**Meets NATEF Task**: (A8-A-3) Research the vehicle and service information, vehicle history and TSBs. (P-1)

Name _____  Date _____  Time on Task _____

Make/Model _____  Year _____  Evaluation: 4  3  2  1

_____ 1. Vehicle and/or electrical-related technical service bulletins (TSBs).

    A. Topic _____  Bulletin number _____
    Problem/correction _____

    B. Topic _____  Bulletin number _____
    Problem/correction _____

    C. Topic _____  Bulletin number _____
    Problem/correction _____

    D. Topic _____  Bulletin number _____
    Problem/correction _____

_____ 2. Vehicle history of repair. List all repairs from customer records or repair order files.
    _____
    _____

_____ 3. List all engine performance-related service precautions as published in service information.

    A. _____  E. _____
    B. _____  F. _____
    C. _____  G. _____
    D. _____  H. _____

_____ 4. Determine the location of the following electrical service information and where (books, CD, Web site) it was found.

    A. Spark plug torque specifications: _____  Located _____
    B. Fuel system pressure specifications: _____  Located _____
    C. Charging system voltage specified _____  Located _____
    D. Other (specify) _____  Located _____

# Vehicle Service History

**Meets NATEF Task:** (A8-A-3) Research vehicle service information, vehicle service history and TSBs. (P-1)

Name _____ Date _____ Time on Task _____

Make/Model _____ Year _____ Evaluation: 4  3  2  1

_____ **1.** Search vehicle history (check all that apply).

_____ Computerized data base (electronic file if previous service work)

_____ Files (hard copy of previous service work)

_____ Customer information (verbal)

_____ Other (describe) _____

_____ **2.** What engine performance-related repairs have been performed in this vehicle?

_____

_____

_____

_____

_____ **3.** From the information obtained, has the vehicle been serviced regularly?

_____ Yes (describe the service intervals) _____

_____

_____

_____ No (why?) _____

_____

_____ **4.** Based on the service history information, is the service record helpful? Why or why not? _____

_____

_____

# Technical Service Bulletins

**Meets NATEF Task:** (A8-A-3) Research vehicle service information, vehicle service history and TSBs. (P-1)

Name _____ Date _____ Time on Task _____

Make/Model _____ Year _____ Evaluation:  4  3  2  1

_____ **1.** Technical service bulletins can be accessed through (check all that apply):

_____ Internet site(s), specify _____

_____ Paper bulletins, specify source _____

_____ CD ROM bulletins, specify source _____

_____ Other (describe) _____

_____ **2.** List all electrical-related technical service bulletins that pertain to the vehicle/engine being serviced.

| Number | Description/Correction |
|---|---|
| _____ | _____ |
| _____ | _____ |
| _____ | _____ |
| _____ | _____ |

_____ **3.** Based on this research, is the information located helpful?

_____ Yes, why? _____

_____ No, why not? _____

# VIN Code

**Meets NATEF Task:** (A8-A-4) Locate and interpret vehicle identification numbers. (P-1)

Name _____   Date _____   Time on Task _____

Make/Model _____   Year _____   Evaluation:  4  3  2  1

VIN Number _____

- The first number or letter designates the **country of origin** = _____

| | | | |
|---|---|---|---|
| 1 = United States | 6 = Australia | L = China | V = France |
| 2 = Canada | 8 = Argentina | R = Taiwan | W = Germany |
| 3 = Mexico | 9 = Brazil | S = England | X = Russia |
| 4 = United States | J = Japan | T = Czechoslovakia | Y = Sweden |
| 5 = United States | K = Korea | U = Romania | Z = Italy |

- The model of the vehicle is commonly the fourth or fifth character. **Model?** _____

- The eighth character is often the engine code. (Some engines cannot be determined by the VIN number.) **Engine code:** _____

- The tenth character represents the year on all vehicles. See the following chart.

**VIN Year Chart** (The pattern repeats every 30 years.)      **Year?** _____

| | | | |
|---|---|---|---|
| A = 1980/2010 | J = 1988/2018 | T = 1996/2026 | 4 = 2004/2034 |
| B = 1981/2011 | K = 1989/2019 | V = 1997/2027 | 5 = 2005/2035 |
| C = 1982/2012 | L = 1990/2020 | W = 1998/2028 | 6 = 2006/2036 |
| D = 1983/2013 | M = 1991/2021 | X = 1999/2029 | 7 = 2007/2037 |
| E = 1984/2014 | N = 1992/2022 | Y = 2000/2030 | 8 = 2008/2038 |
| F = 1985/2015 | P = 1993/2023 | 1 = 2001/2031 | 9 = 2009/2039 |
| G = 1986/2016 | R = 1994/2024 | 2 = 2002/2032 | |
| H = 1987/2017 | S = 1995/2025 | 3 = 2003/2033 | |

# 9

# Vehicle Safety Certification Label

**Meets NATEF Task:** (A8-A-4) Locate and interpret vehicle and major component identification numbers. (P-1)

---

Name _____ Date _____ Time on Task _____

Make/Model _____ Year _____ Evaluation: 4  3  2  1

_____ 1. Describe the location of the Vehicle Safety Certification Label (usually located on the driver's side pillar post).

_____

MFD BY GENERAL MOTORS OF CANADA LTD.

**GM**

| DATE | GVWR | GAWR FRT | GAWR RR |
|------|------|----------|---------|
| 06/02 | 2071 KG | 1115 KG | 956 KG |
| | 4565 LB | 2458 LB | 2107 LB |

THIS VEHICLE CONFORMS TO ALL APPLICABLE U.S. FEDERAL MOTOR VEHICLE SAFETY, BUMPER, AND THEFT PREVENTION STANDARDS IN EFFECT ON THE DATE OF MANUFACTURE SHOWN ABOVE.

2G1WF52E839104270     TYPE: PASS CAR

_____ 2. What is the month and year the vehicle was manufactured?

Month = _____

Year = _____

_____ 3. What is the gross vehicle weight rating (GVWR)?

_____

_____ 4. What is the gross axle weight rating (GAWR)?

_____

_____ 5. Is the exact date of manufacture listed on the label?

____ Yes     Month = _____     Day = _____     Year = _____

____ No

# 10

# Hybrid High-Voltage Disconnect

**Meets NATEF Task:** (A6-A-21) Identify the location of hybrid vehicle safety disconnect location and safety procedures. (P-3)

Name _____ Date _____ Time on Task _____

Make/Model _____ Year _____ Evaluation: 4 3 2 1

**Hybrid electric vehicles (HEV)** use a high-voltage battery pack and an electric motor(s) to help propel the vehicle. To safely work around a hybrid electric vehicle, the high-voltage (HV) battery and circuits should be shut off following these steps:

**Step 1**      Turn off the ignition key (if equipped) and remove the key from the ignition switch.

**Step 2**      Disconnect the high-voltage circuits.

> **CAUTION:** Some vehicle manufacturers specify that rubber insulated lineman's gloves be used whenever working around the high-voltage circuits to prevent the danger of electrical shock.

**Toyota Prius**

The cutoff switch is located in the trunk. To gain access, remove three clips holding the upper left portion of the trunk side cover. To disconnect the high-voltage system, pull the orange handled plug while wearing insulated rubber lineman's gloves.

**Ford Escape**

The high-voltage shut off switch is located in the rear of the vehicle under the right side carpet.

**Honda Civic**

To totally disable the high-voltage system on a Honda Civic, remove the main fuse (labeled number 1) from the driver's side underhood fuse panel.

**Chevrolet/GMC Pickup Truck**

The high-voltage shut off switch is located under the rear passenger seat. Remove the cover marked "energy storage box" and turn the green service disconnect switch to the horizontal position to turn off the high-voltage circuits.

# 11

# Material Safety Data Sheet (MSDS)

**Meets NATEF Task:** Environmental safety practices for engine performance (A8).

Name _____ Date _____ Time on Task _____

Make/Model _____ Year _____ Evaluation: 4 3 2 1

_____ **1.** Locate the MSDS sheets and describe their location

_____

_____

• **Product name** _____

        chemical name(s)

        _____

        Does the chemical contain "chlor" or "fluor" which may indicate hazardous

        materials? **Yes** _____ **No** _____

        flash point = _____ (hopefully above 140° F)

        pH _____ (7 = neutral, higher than 7 = caustic (base), lower than 7 = acid)

• **Product name** _____

        chemical name(s) _____

        Does the chemical contain "chlor" or "fluor" which may indicate hazardous

        materials? **Yes** _____ **No** _____

        flash point = _____ (hopefully above 140° F)

        pH _____ (7 = neutral, higher than 7 = caustic (base), lower than 7 = acid)

• **Product name** _____

        chemical name(s) _____

        Does the chemical contain "chlor" or "fluor" which may indicate hazardous

        materials? **Yes** _____ **No** _____

        flash point = _____ (hopefully above 140° F)

        pH _____ (7 = neutral, higher than 7 = caustic (base), lower than 7 = acid)

# 12

# Gasoline Engine Identification

**Meets NATEF Task:** (A8-A-4) Locate and interpret vehicle and major component identification information. (P-1)

Name _____ Date _____ Time on Task _____

Make/Model _____ Year _____ Evaluation: 4 3 2 1

_____ 1. Number of cylinders = _____ Arrangement of cylinders = _____

_____ 2. Number and arrangement of camshafts = _____

_____ 3. Bore = _____ Stroke = _____ Cu. in. = _____ cc = _____ Liters = _____

_____ 4. Rated HP = _____ @ RPM _____

_____ 5. Rated torque = _____ @ RPM _____

_____ 6. Compression ratio = _____

_____ 7. Recommended octane of gasoline required = _____

_____ 8. The block is constructed of: _____ cast iron _____ aluminum

_____ 9. Cylinder head(s) is constructed of: _____ cast iron _____ aluminum

_____ 10. Intake manifold is: _____ one piece _____ two pieces (upper and lower) and is
constructed of: _____ cast iron _____ aluminum _____ composite

_____ 11. Casting numbers on the block _____ Cylinder head(s) _____
Crankshaft _____

# 13

# General Engine Specification

**Meets NATEF Task:** (A8-A-4) Locate and interpret vehicle and major component
identification numbers. (P-1)

Name _____ Date _____ Time on Task _____

Make/Model _____ Year _____ Evaluation: 4  3  2  1

_____ 1. Engine type (V-6, V-8, etc.) = _____

_____ 2. Bore = _____

_____ 3. Stroke = _____

_____ 4. Compression ratio = _____

_____ 5. Displacement: cubic inches = _____

            cc = _____ liter = _____

_____ 6. Horsepower = _____ @ _____ RPM

_____ 7. Torque = _____ @ _____ RPM

_____ 8. Firing order = _____

_____ 9. Engine oil capacity = _____

_____ 10. Cylinder block material = _____

_____ 11. Crankshaft material (forged steel, cast iron) = _____

_____ 12. Cylinder head material = _____

_____ 13. Connecting rod material (forged steel, powdered metal, etc.) = _____

# 14

# Diesel Engine Identification

**Meets NATEF Task:** (A8-A-4) Locate and interpret vehicle and major component identification numbers (VIN, vehicle certification labels, and calibration decals). (P-1)

Name _____ Date _____ Time on Task _____

Make/Model _____ Year _____ Evaluation: 4 3 2 1

Check service information and determine the following information.

_____ 1. Compression ratio = _____

_____ 2. Fuel pressure (lift pump) = _____

_____ 3. Fuel pressure (common rail) = _____

_____ 4. Oil viscosity required = _____

_____ 5. Bore = _____

_____ 6. Stroke = _____

_____ 7. Cubic inch displacement = _____

_____ 8. Cubic centimeter displacement = _____

_____ 9. Liter displacement = _____

_____ 10. Fuel filter replacement interval = _____

_____ 11. Air filter replacement interval = _____

_____ 12. Oil change interval = _____

_____ 13. Horsepower @ RPM = _____ @ _____RPM

_____ 14. Torque @ RPM = _____ @ _____ RPM

_____ 15. Maximum engine speed _____

# Diesel Engine Emission Control Systems

**Meets NATEF Task:** (A8-A-4) Locate and interpret vehicle and major component identification numbers (VIN, vehicle certification labels, and calibration decals). (P-1)

Name _____ Date _____ Time on Task _____

Make/Model _____ Year _____ Evaluation: 4  3  2  1

_____ **1.** Check the vehicle emission control information (VECI) underhood sticker and determine which of the following emission control devices are used. (Check all that apply.)

      _____ EGR

      _____ PCV

      _____ DPE

      _____ Other (describe) _____

_____ **2.** Is the engine equipped with an electronic throttle control (ETC) system?

      Yes _____ No _____

_____ **3.** Is the engine equipped with a throttle plate to help control EGR?

      Yes _____ No _____ If yes, describe the location: _____

_____ **4.** Are the EGR gases cooled before they enter the engine?

      Yes _____ No _____ If yes, describe the method of cooling and the location:

      _____

# 16

# Gasoline Retailer Information

**Meets NATEF Task:** (None specified for this activity.)

---

**Name** _____ **Date** _____ **Time on Task** _____

**Make/Model** _____ **Year** _____ **Evaluation:  4  3  2  1**

Visit three gasoline stations and record the following information about the available fuels in your area.

**Station #1**  List the name brand and location: _____

Regular octane rating posted _____ Price per gallon _____
Plus (midgrade) octane rating posted _____ Price per gallon _____
Premium octane rating posted _____ Price per gallon _____
Other (describe) _____ _____ Price per gallon _____
Ethanol 10% _____ Yes _____ No _____ Unknown
E-85 _____ Yes _____ No _____ Unknown
Reformulated? _____ Yes _____ No _____ Unknown
Low sulfur? _____ Yes _____ No _____ Unknown

**Station #2**  List the name brand and location: _____

Regular octane rating posted _____ Price per gallon _____
Plus (midgrade) octane rating posted _____ Price per gallon _____
Premium octane rating posted _____ Price per gallon _____
Other (describe) _____ _____ Price per gallon _____
Ethanol 10% _____ Yes _____ No _____ Unknown
E-85 _____ Yes _____ No _____ Unknown
Reformulated? _____ Yes _____ No _____ Unknown
Low sulfur? _____ Yes _____ No _____ Unknown

**Station #3**  List the name brand and location: _____

Regular octane rating posted _____ Price per gallon _____
Plus (midgrade) octane rating posted _____ Price per gallon _____
Premium octane rating posted _____ Price per gallon _____
Other (describe) _____ _____ Price per gallon _____
Ethanol 10% _____ Yes _____ No _____ Unknown
E-85 _____ Yes _____ No _____ Unknown
Reformulated? _____ Yes _____ No _____ Unknown
Low sulfur? _____ Yes _____ No _____ Unknown

# 17

# Vehicle Fuel Specification

**Meets NATEF Task:** (A8-A-3) Research vehicle and service information.
(P-1)

---

Name _____ Date _____ Time on Task _____

Make/Model _____ Year _____ Evaluation: 4 3 2 1

_____ **1.** Using service information, list three vehicles that require the use of regular (87 octane) unleaded gasoline.

        A. _____

        B. _____

        C. _____

_____ **2.** Using service information, list three vehicles that require the use of premium (91+ octane) unleaded gasoline.

        A. _____

        B. _____

        C. _____

MEETS MICH. QUALITY & PURITY STANDARDS FOR
**UNLEADED MIDGRADE 89
CONTAINS: ETHANOL 10%**
CONSUMER COMPLAINT TOLL-FREE HOT LINE:
CALL 1-800-MDA FUEL

_____ **3.** List any vehicle that is required to use midgrade (plus or 89 octane) unleaded gasoline.

        _____

_____ **4.** Are the three vehicles listed in #1 above able to use ethanol up to 10%?

        _____ Yes _____ No (list those that cannot) _____

        _____

_____ **5.** Are the three vehicles listed in #1 above able to use MTBE up to 15%?

        _____ Yes _____ No (list those that cannot) _____

        _____

# 18

# Fuel-Related Scan Data

**Meets NATEF Task:** (A8-B-7) Diagnose driveability and emissions problems resulting from malfunctions of interrelated systems. (P-3)

---

Name _____ Date _____ Time on Task _____

Make/Model _____ Year _____ Evaluation: 4  3  2  1

_____ 1. Check service information for the specified octane rating and/or alcohol type to be used.

Recommended octane of gasoline = _____

Recommended alcohol type and percentage (if equipped for alcohol or flexible fuel use) = _____

_____ 2. Connect a scan tool to the data link connector and check for fuel-related data. Check all that apply.

**NOTE:** Use the vehicle specific or enhanced version to get the most information from the vehicle.

_____ Calculated octane

_____ Gallons of fuel remaining

_____ Percentage of alcohol in the fuel (flexible fuel vehicle)

_____ Fuel pressure

_____ Fuel temperature

_____ Other (list and/or describe) _____

```
OBD II FUNCTIONS

F1: DATA LIST
F2: DTCs
F3: SNAPSHOT
F4: OBD CONTROLS
F5: SYSTEM TESTS
F6: OBD EVALUATIONS
F8: INFORMATION
F9: UNIT CONVERSION
```

_____ 3. Based on the results of the information obtained and the specification for the vehicle, what is the interpretation of the data?

_____

_____

# 19

# Alcohol Content in Gasoline

**Meets NATEF Task:** (A8-D-2) Check fuel for contaminants and quality; determine necessary action. (P-2)

Name _____ Date _____ Time on Task _____

Make/Model _____ Year _____ Evaluation: 4  3  2  1

Take the following steps when testing gasoline for alcohol content.

_____ 1. Pour suspect gasoline into a small clean beaker or glass container.

**DO NOT SMOKE OR RUN THE TEST AROUND SOURCES OF IGNITION!**

_____ 2. Carefully fill the graduated cylinder to the 10-mL mark.

_____ 3. Add 2 mL of water to the graduated cylinder by counting the number of drops from an eyedropper. (Before performing the test, the eyedropper must be calibrated to determine how many drops equal 2.0 mL.)

_____ 4. Put the stopper in the cylinder and shake vigorously for 1 minute. Relieve built-up pressure by occasionally removing the stopper. Alcohol dissolves in water and will drop to the bottom of the cylinder.

_____ 5. Place the cylinder on a flat surface and let it stand for 2 minutes.

_____ 6. Take a reading near the bottom of the cylinder at the boundary between the two liquids.

_____ 7. For percent of alcohol in gasoline, subtract 2 from the reading and multiply by 10.

For example,   The reading is 3.1 mL:  $3.1 - 2 = 1.1 \times 10 = 11\%$ alcohol

The reading is 2.0 mL:  $2 - 2 = 0 \times 10 = 0\%$ alcohol (no alcohol)

If the increase in volume is 0.2% or less, it may be assumed that the test gasoline contains no alcohol. Alcohol content can also be checked using an electronic tester.

_____ 8. Based on the test results, what action is necessary? _____

_____

_____

_____

# 20

# Fuel Composition Tester

**Meets NATEF Task:** (A8-D-2) Check fuel for contaminants and quality; determine necessary action. (P-2)

Name _____ Date _____ Time on Task _____

Make/Model _____ Year _____ Evaluation: 4  3  2  1

A fuel composition tester is used to determine the percentage of alcohol in a gasoline sample.

_____ 1. Check service information for the specified method of taking a fuel sample from the vehicle.

_____

_____

_____ 2. Follow the instructions of the tester to determine the alcohol content of the gasoline. The normal procedure for one type of tester states:

a. Connect a DMM and set to read AC Hertz. Verify the proper tool and meter hookup by checking the air frequency (normally between 35 and 48 Hertz).

b. Pour the sample gasoline into the testing cell of the tool.

c. Record the AC frequency of the sample and subtract 50. The number that results is the percentage of alcohol.

_____ 3. What is the air frequency? _____

_____ 4. What is the frequency of the gasoline sample? _____

_____ 5. Subtract 50 from the number in #4. What is the alcohol content of the gasoline sample?

_____

_____ 6. Based on this test, what action is necessary?

_____

_____

_____

# 21

# Gasoline Reid Vapor Pressure

**Meets NATEF Task:** (A8-D-2) Check fuel for contaminants and quality; determine necessary action. (P-2)

---

**Name** _____     **Date** _____     **Time on Task** _____

**Make/Model** _____     **Year** _____     **Evaluation:** 4  3  2  1

_____ **1.** Check service information for the recommended Reid vapor pressure (RVP) of the

gasoline to be used.

What is the RVP recommended?

_____ Summer grade _____

_____ Winter grade _____

_____ Not available

_____ **2.** Using the standardized test procedure to determine the vapor pressure of fuel at 100°F,

what is the RVP?

_____

_____

_____

_____

_____

_____ **3.** Based on the factory specifications and test results, what is the necessary action?

_____

_____

# 22

# Alternative Fuel

**Meets NATEF Task:** None Specified

---

**Name** _____ **Date** _____ **Time on Task** _____

**Make/Model** _____ **Year** _____ **Evaluation: 4 3 2 1**

_____ **1.** Check service information to determine how to identify if the vehicle is able to use an
alternative fuel. What VIN or other identification indicates that the vehicle is able to
use an alternative fuel? _____

_____

_____ **2.** What fuel can be used? (check all that apply)

    _____ Gasoline

    _____ E10 (10% ethanol, 90% gasoline)

    _____ E85 (85% ethanol, 15% gasoline)

    _____ M85 (85% methanol, 15% gasoline)

    _____ Propane (LPG)

    _____ Compressed natural gas (CNG)

    _____ LNG (liquefied natural gas)

    _____ Other (describe) _____

_____ **3.** What precautions are included in service information if the vehicle is using an
alternative fuel? _____

_____

_____

# 23

# Diesel Fuel

**Meets NATEF Task:** None Specified

Name _____   Date _____   Time on Task _____

Make/Model _____   Year _____   Evaluation:  4  3  2  1

_____ 1. Check service information for the specification of the recommended fuel to use. The recommended fuel should have:

      _____ Cetane rating _____

      _____ Cloud point _____

      _____ Other (describe) _____

_____ 2. What additive, if any, is recommended for use in normal service?

      _____

      _____

      _____

      _____

      _____

> **LOW SULFUR HIGHWAY DIESEL FUEL**
> (500 ppm Sulfur Maximum)
>
> **WARNING**
> Federal law *prohibits* use in model year 2007 and later highway vehicles and engines.
> Its use may damage these vehicles and engines.

_____ 3. What additive, if any, is recommended for use in cold weather? _____

      _____

      _____

_____ 4. What additives, if any, are recommended if the diesel fuel is to be stored or left in a vehicle for longer than a few weeks?

      _____

      _____

      _____

# 24

# Biodiesel Fuel

**Meets NATEF Task:** None Specified

___

**Name** _____ **Date** _____ **Time on Task** _____

**Make/Model** _____ **Year** _____ **Evaluation:** 4 3 2 1

_____ 1. Check service information to determine what percentage of biodiesel is recommended
for use. Check all that apply:

_____ Biodiesel not recommended

_____ B5 (state any restrictions) _____

_____ B20 (state any restrictions) _____

_____ Other (describe) _____

_____ 2. List places where biodiesel can be purchased in your area.

_____

_____

_____

_____

_____ 3. What is the cost difference between biodiesel
and regular diesel fuel?

_____

_____

_____

_____

_____

_____

# 25

# Port Fuel-Injection Intake Manifold Identification

**Meets NATEF Task:** Not specified by NATEF

Name _____ Date _____ Time on Task _____

Make/Model _____ Year _____ Evaluation: 4 3 2 1

_____ **1.** The intake manifold (plenum) is a:

       _____ one-piece design

       _____ two-piece design

       _____ more than two pieces

_____ **2.** The manifold (plenum) is

constructed of:

       _____ plastic

       _____ aluminum

       _____ composite (more than

       one material)

_____ **3.** The engine has:

       _____ one intake valve per cylinder

       _____ two intake valves per cylinder

       _____ three intake valves per cylinder

_____ **4.** The throttle body is:

       _____ a separate replaceable part

       _____ part of the intake manifold

_____ **5.** The manifold includes a manifold tuning valve.

       _____ **Yes**

       _____ **No**

_____ **6.** The fuel rails for the injector are:

       _____ plastic

       _____ metal

# 26

# Exhaust Manifold Identification

**Meets NATEF Task:** Not specified by NATEF

**Name** _____ **Date** _____ **Time on Task** _____

**Make/Model** _____ **Year** _____ **Evaluation:** 4   3   2   1

_____ 1. Number of exhaust manifolds on the engine?

       _____ one
       _____ two

_____ 2. Type of material used?

       _____ cast iron
       _____ steel (header-type manifold)
       _____ other (describe)

_____

_____ 3. Exhaust manifold(s) laminated (two pieces sandwiched together)?

       **Yes** _____   **No** _____

_____ 4. Is there a gasket used between the exhaust manifold and the cylinder head from the factory?

       **Yes** _____   **No** _____

_____ 5. What type of fasteners are used to hold the exhaust manifold to the cylinder head?

       _____ bolts
       _____ nuts (uses studs in the head)

_____ 6. What is the torque specification for the fasteners?

_____

_____ 7. Carefully inspect the exhaust manifold for cracks or damage.

       **OK** _____   **NOT OK** _____

# 27

# TBI/Carburetor Intake Manifold Identification

**Meets NATEF Task:** Not specified by NATEF

**Name** _____   **Date** _____   **Time on Task** _____

**Make/Model** _____   **Year** _____   **Evaluation: 4  3  2  1**

_____ **1.** The intake manifold is a:

      _____ one-piece design

      _____ two-piece design

      _____ more than two piece

_____ **2.** The manifold is constructed of:

      _____ plastic     _____ aluminum     _____ composite (more than one material)

_____ **3.** The engine uses:

      _____ one intake valve per cylinder

      _____ two intake valves per cylinder

_____ **4.** The intake manifold is equipped with an EGR valve or EGR passages.

      **Yes** _____    **No** _____

_____ **5.** How does the intake manifold heat the air/fuel mixture?

      _____ exhaust crossover passages

      _____ electrically heated grid under the TBI/carburetor

      _____ other (describe) _____

# 28

# Intake Manifold Gasket Replacement

**Meets NATEF Task:** Not specified by NATEF

Name _____ Date _____ Time on Task _____

Make/Model _____ Year _____ Evaluation:  4  3  2  1

An intake manifold gasket will have to be replaced if there is one or more of the following problems:

- An air (vacuum) leak that affects the operation of the engine
- A coolant leak around the cooling passages of the intake manifold
- An oil leak from the gasket area of the intake manifold

_____ 1. Check service information for the specified procedure and fastener torque specified. Describe the procedure. _____

_____

_____ 2. Remove the intake manifold.

_____ 3. Clean the gasket surfaces.

> **CAUTION:** Do not use fiber abrasive pads to clean the gasket surfaces. Particles of the fiber disc can get into the engine and cause serious engine wear and damage. Do not use steel tools to scrape gaskets from an aluminum surface.

_____ 4. Install the replacement gasket(s) and the intake manifold. Torque the retaining bolts to factory specifications.

Intake manifold bolt torque specification = _____

_____ 5. Reassemble the top of the engine.

_____ 6. Refill the cooling system with new coolant.

> **CAUTION:** Be sure to open the cooling system bleeder valves(s), if equipped, to avoid trapping air.

_____ 7. Install the radiator pressure cap and start the engine. Check for leaks and proper cooling system operation.

# 29

# Exhaust System Inspection

**Meets NATEF Task:** (A8-D-5) Inspect throttle body, air induction system, intake manifold and gaskets for vacuum leaks and/or unmetered air. (P-2)

Name _____   Date _____   Time on Task _____

Make/Model _____   Year _____   Evaluation:  4  3  2  1

_____ **1.** Safely hoist the vehicle and wear safety glasses.

_____ **2.** Visually inspect the following items and note their condition.

    Tailpipe            **OK** _____   **NOT OK** _____
    Describe fault: _____

    Muffler             **OK** _____   **NOT OK** _____
    Describe fault: _____

    Exhaust Pipe        **OK** _____   **NOT OK** _____
    Describe fault: _____

    Hangers             **OK** _____   **NOT OK** _____
    Describe fault: _____

    Catalytic converter **OK** _____   **NOT OK** _____
    Describe fault: _____

    Header or Y-pipe    **OK** _____   **NOT OK** _____
    Describe fault: _____

    Exhaust manifold(s) **OK** _____   **NOT OK** _____
    Describe fault: _____

    Heat shields(s)     **OK** _____   **NOT OK** _____
    Describe fault: _____

    Other (describe) _____
    _____

_____ **3.** Based on the inspection, what is the necessary action? _____
    _____

# 30

# Turbocharger Identification

**Meets NATEF Task:** (A8-A-3) Research vehicle information. (P-1)

Name _____ Date _____ Time on Task _____

Make/Model _____ Year _____ Evaluation: 4 3 2 1

_____ **1.** Check service information and determine the following information:

    a. Location of the turbocharger (describe): _____

    _____

    b. Is the turbo system equipped with an intercooler? Yes _____ No _____

       If yes, describe the location and type (air-to-air or air-to-liquid) _____

    _____

    c. Type of turbocharger control includes (check all that apply):

      ___ 1. Wastegate

      ___ 2. Blow off valve

      ___ 3. Variable vane

    d. Are the turbocharger bushings liquid cooled? Yes _____ No _____

    e. What is the recommended oil change interval and specified engine oil?

      Recommended oil change interval: _____

      Recommended engine oil specification: _____

_____ **2.** Check turbocharger and verify that all components are free of defects, including hoses and hose clamps.

    **OK** _____ **Not OK** _____

    (describe faults) _____

    _____

    _____

# 31

# Supercharger Identification

**Meets NATEF Task:** (A8-A-3) Research vehicle information. (P-1)

---

**Name** _____ **Date** _____ **Time on Task** _____

**Make/Model** _____ **Year** _____ **Evaluation:** 4  3  2  1

_____ 1. Check service information and determine the following information:

    a. Location of supercharger: (describe) _____

        _____

    b. Type of boost control? (describe) _____

        _____

    c. Does the supercharger system use an intercooler?  Yes _____  No _____

        If yes, describe the location and type (air-to-air or air-to-liquid): _____

        _____

    d. How is the supercharger unit lubricated?  (describe) _____

        _____

    e. What is the recommended oil and oil change interval?

        Recommended oil _____

        Recommended oil change interval _____

_____ 2. Check the supercharger and verify that all components are free from defects, including drive belt and hoses/clamps.  **OK** _____  **Not OK** _____  If not OK, describe the faults: _____

_____

_____

_____

_____

_____

# 32

# Turbocharger/Supercharger Diagnosis

**Meets NATEF Task:** (A8-D-10) Test the operation of turbocharger/supercharger systems; determine necessary action. (P-3)

Name _____ Date _____ Time on Task _____

Make/Model _____ Year _____ Evaluation:  4  3  2  1

_____ **1.** The vehicle is equipped with which system?

        _____ Turbocharger (exhaust driven)

        _____ Supercharger (engine driven)

_____ **2.** Check service information for the exact procedure to follow to determine the correct operation of the turbocharger/supercharger. Describe the inspection procedure.

        _____

        _____

        _____

_____ **3.** Based on the specified test and inspection procedures, what is the necessary action?

        _____

        _____

        _____

# 33

# Engine Problem Analysis

**Meets NATEF Task:** (A1-A-2) Identify and interpret engine concern; determine necessary action. (P-1)

---

Name _____ Date _____ Time on Task _____

Make/Model _____ Year _____ Evaluation: 4  3  2  1

_____ 1. State the customer's concern regarding the engine problem. _____

_____

    A. Excessive noise? _____

    Describe: _____

    B. Exhaust smoke? _____

_____

    C. Engine operation (missing, runs rough, etc.)? Describe: _____

_____

_____ 2. Based on the symptoms described above, what tests should be performed?

    ____ Compression test

    ____ Cylinder linkage test

    ____ Power balance test

    ____ Other (describe): _____

_____ 3. Based on the symptoms and the test results, what is the necessary action?

_____

_____

_____

# 34

# Fluid Leakage Detection

**Meets NATEF Task:** (A8-A-5) Inspect engine for fuel, oil, coolant and other leaks; determine necessary action (P-2)

---

**Name** _____ **Date** _____ **Time on Task** _____

**Make/Model** _____ **Year** _____ **Evaluation:** 4  3  2  1

_____ **1.** Check the fuel system for leaks from the fuel tank to the intake manifold.

     A. Visually check for leaks

         _____ OK – Nothing found visually

         _____ NOT OK – Found the leak – Describe the location: _____

         _____

     B. Smell test for leaks

         _____ OK – Did not smell fuel at any location

         _____ NOT OK – Smelled fuel – Describe the location: _____

         _____

     C. Hydrocarbon test for leaks

         _____ OK – Detector did not indicate any leaks

         _____ NOT OK – Fuel leak detected – Describe the location: _____

         _____

_____ **2.** Based on the inspection for fuel leaks, what is the necessary action? _____

_____

_____

# 35

# Head Gasket Diagnosis

**Meets NATEF Task:** (A8-A-5) Inspect engine assembly for fuel, oil, coolant, and other leaks; determine necessary action. (P-2)

---

Name _____ Date _____ Time on Task _____

Make/Model _____ Year _____ Evaluation: 4 3 2 1

A blown (defective) head gasket is often difficult to diagnose. To verify that a head gasket is defective, perform the following tests and checks.

_____ 1. Is excessive white steam visual at the tail pipe (disregard normal steam that occurs in cold weather)?

         **OK** _____     **NOT OK** _____

_____ 2. Check for visual signs of coolant or oil leakage between the block and the cylinder head.

         **OK** _____     **NOT OK** _____

_____ 3. Is the level of coolant lower than normal? (Lower than normal coolant level can indicate a defective head gasket.)

         **OK** _____     **NOT OK** _____

_____ 4. Does the engine run correctly (a blown head gasket often causes the engine to miss)?

         **OK** _____     **NOT OK** _____

_____ 5. Remove the radiator cap after the engine has cooled and use an exhaust gas analysis kit to determine whether exhaust gases are present in the coolant. One common test involves drawing coolant into a container with blue liquid in it and if it changes color to a yellow/green, then exhaust gases are present in the coolant.

         **OK** _____     **NOT OK** _____

_____ 6. Start the engine and use a 4- or 5-gas analyzer to check for CO and/or HC emissions above the open radiator cap.

         **OK** _____     **NOT OK** _____

_____ 7. Based on the tests results, what is the necessary action? _____

_____

# 36

# Engine Noise Diagnosis

**Meets NATEF Task:** (A8-A-6) Diagnose abnormal engine noise or vibration concerns; determine necessary action  (P-3)

Name _____   Date _____   Time on Task _____

Make/Model _____   Year _____   Evaluation:  4   3   2   1

Analyzing engine noise helps determine the extent of needed repairs. Some noises are easy to correct, whereas other noises may represent extensive and expensive repairs.

_____ 1.  When does the noise occur?

        _____ at start up (cold engine only)

        _____ at start up (all the time)

        _____ cold engine only

        _____ warm engine only

        _____ all the time

        _____ other (describe)

_____

_____ 2.  What does the noise sound like?

        _____ Clicking noise - like the clicking of a ballpoint pen

        _____ Clacking noise - like tapping on metal

        _____ Knock - like knocking on a door

        _____ Rattle - like a baby rattle

        _____ Clatter - like rolling marbles

        _____ Whine - like an electric motor running

        _____ Clunk - like a door closing

_____ 3.  Based on the noise, what is the necessary action?

_____

_____

# 37

# Abnormal Exhaust Color, Odor, or Sound

**Meets NATEF Task:** (A8-A-7) Diagnose abnormal exhaust color, odor, and sound; determine necessary action. (P-2)

Name _____ Date _____ Time on Task _____

Make/Model _____ Year _____ Evaluation: 4 3 2 1

_____ 1. Check the vehicle for abnormal exhaust color, odor, and sound. (check all that apply)

_____ Abnormal exhaust color (describe) _____
_____

_____ Abnormal exhaust odor (describe) _____
_____

_____ Abnormal exhaust sound (describe) _____
_____

_____ 2. Check service information to determine what steps should be followed. Describe the specified instructions.

_____
_____

_____ 3. Based on the test results, what is the necessary action?

_____
_____

# 38

# Vacuum Testing

**Meets NATEF Task:** (A8-A-8) Perform engine absolute (vacuum/boost) manifold pressure tests; determine necessary action (P-1)

Name _____   Date _____   Time on Task _____

Make/Model _____   Year _____   Evaluation:  4  3  2  1

_____ 1. Connect the vacuum gauge to a manifold vacuum source (source of vacuum at idle).

_____ 2. Vacuum at idle = _____ in. Hg.   (should be 17-21 in. Hg. and steady).

_____ 3. Drive the vehicle on a level road in high gear at a steady speed.

        Cruise vacuum = _____ in. Hg.   (should be 10-15 in. Hg.)

_____ 4. Accelerate the vehicle in high gear to W.O.T.

        W.O.T. vacuum = _____ in. Hg.   (should be almost zero)

_____ 5. Decelerate the vehicle from 50 MPH with the throttle closed.

        Deceleration vacuum = _____ in. Hg.   (should be higher than idle vacuum)

_____ 6. With the engine out of gear and the brake firmly applied, raise the engine speed to 2,000 RPM and hold for one full minute. This tests for an exhaust restriction.

        Results = _____ in. Hg.

_____ 7. Stop the engine. Disable the ignition. Crank the engine and observe the vacuum during cranking.

        Cranking vacuum = _____ in. Hg.   (should be higher than 2.5 in. Hg.)

        **OK_____**          **NOT OK_____**

_____ 8. Based on the vacuum test results, what is the necessary action? _____

_____

# 39

# Cylinder Power Balance Tests

**Meets NATEF Task**: (A8-A-9) Perform cylinder power balance tests; determine necessary action. (P-2)

---

Name _____ Date _____ Time on Task _____

Make/Model _____ Year _____ Evaluation: 4 3 2 1

_____ 1. An automotive diagnostic scope or digital storage oscilloscope with relative compression can be used to determine cylinder balance. Check all that apply.

      _____ Automotive diagnostic scope
      _____ Digital storage oscilloscope with relative compression capability
      _____ Other (describe) _____

_____ 2. Follow the equipment manufacturers' instructions and connect the tester to the engine. Instructions to connect to the engine include: _____

_____

_____ 3. Start the engine and allow it to reach normal operating temperature.

_____ 4. Follow the instructions of the test equipment manufacturer and perform a cylinder power balance test. Record the results.

      Cylinder #1 = _____     Cylinder #5 = _____
      Cylinder #2 = _____     Cylinder #6 = _____
      Cylinder #3 = _____     Cylinder #7 = _____
      Cylinder #4 = _____     Cylinder #8 = _____

_____ 5. If performing an engine speed (RPM) drop test, all cylinders should be within 50 RPM.

      _____ **OK**
      _____ **NOT OK** (describe results) _____
      _____ **NA**

_____ 6. If relative compression is being performed, all cylinders should be within 10%.

      _____ **OK**
      _____ **NOT OK** (describe results) _____
      _____ **NA**

# 40

# Compression Testing

**Meets NATEF Task:** (A8-A-10) Perform cylinder compression tests; determine necessary action (P-1)

Name _____ Date _____ Time on Task _____

Make/Model _____ Year _____ Evaluation: 4 3 2 1

_____ **1.** Remove all spark plugs (be certain to label the spark plug wires) and disable the ignition system to avoid possible ignition coil damage.

_____ **2.** Block open the throttle and choke (if equipped).

_____ **3.** Crank the engine at least 4 "puffs" (compression strokes) while observing the gauge.

> **NOTE:** For accurate test results, the engine should be at normal operating temperature.

**RESULTS:** 1st puff / final reading    1st puff / final reading

1. _____ / _____    5. _____ / _____
2. _____ / _____    6. _____ / _____
3. _____ / _____    7. _____ / _____
4. _____ / _____    8. _____ / _____

> **NOTE:** The 1st "puff" should be more than one-half of the pressure of the final puff. If the 1st puff is low, worn piston rings are likely – repeat the test.

_____ **4.** Reinstall all spark plugs except one. Perform a running compression test at idle and at 2000 RPM for each cylinder:

| Idle | 2000 RPM |
|---|---|
| 1. _____ | 1. _____ |
| 2. _____ | 2. _____ |
| 3. _____ | 3. _____ |
| 4. _____ | 4. _____ |
| 5. _____ | 5. _____ |
| 6. _____ | 6. _____ |
| 7. _____ | 7. _____ |
| 8. _____ | 8. _____ |

OK_____    NOT OK_____

_____ **5.** Based on the test results, what is the necessary action? _____

_____

# 41

# Cylinder Leakage Test

**Meets NATEF Task:** (A8-A-11) Perform cylinder leakage tests; determine necessary action. (P-1)

---

Name _____ Date _____ Time on Task _____

Make/Model _____ Year _____ Evaluation:  4  3  2  1


_____ **1.** The engine should be at normal operating temperature.

_____ **2.** Rotate the engine until the piston of the cylinder being tested is at TDC on the compression stroke.

_____ **3.** Calibrate the cylinder leakage gauge.

_____ **4.** Install compressed air in the cylinder.  Read the gauge.

_____ % of leakage

**Check one:**

_____ **Good** - less than 10%

_____ **Acceptable** - less than 20%

_____ **Unacceptable** - higher than 20%

_____ **5.** Check the *source* of air leakage:

_____ a. **radiator** - possible blown head gasket or cracked cylinder head.

_____ b. **tail pipe** - defective exhaust valve(s).

_____ c. **carburetor or air inlet** - defective intake valve(s).

_____ d. **oil filler cap** - possible worn or defective piston rings.

_____ **6.** Based on the test results, what is the necessary action? _____

_____

# 42

# Oil Pressure Measurement

**Meets NATEF Task:** (A8-A-12) Diagnose engine mechanical, electrical, electronic, fuel, and ignition concerns; determine necessary action. (P-1)

---

Name _____ Date _____ Time on Task _____

Make/Model _____ Year _____ Evaluation: 4 3 2 1

_____ **1.** Locate the oil pressure-sending (sender) unit.

_____ **2.** Remove the sending unit using the proper size sending unit socket or wrench.

_____ **3.** Thread a mechanical oil pressure gauge into the thread portion of the engine block where the sending unit was located.

_____ **4.** Route the oil pressure gauge hose away from the moving components of the engine.

_____ **5.** Start the engine and check for leaks.

_____ **6.** Record the oil pressure:

       oil pressure @ idle _____

       oil pressure @ 1,000 RPM _____

       oil pressure @ 2,000 RPM _____

       oil pressure @ 3,000 RPM _____

       **NOTE**: Most engines require about 10 psi per 1,000 RPM.

Oil pressure gauge

Oil pressure sending unit hole

_____ **7.** Results: (check one)

       **great** _____ (over 10 psi per 1,000 RPM)

       **good** _____ (at 10 psi per 1,000 RPM)

       **bad** _____ (less than 10 psi per 1,000 RPM)

_____ **8.** Based on the test results, what is the necessary action? _____

_____

# 43

# Verify Engine Operating Temperature

**Meets NATEF Task:** (A8-A-14) Verify engine operating temperature; determine necessary action. (P-1)

Name _____  Date _____  Time on Task _____

Make/Model _____  Year _____  Evaluation:  4  3  2  1

_____ **1.** Check service information for specified engine operating temperature, which is generally between the thermostat temperature rating and 20°F above the thermostat temperature.

Thermostat temperature = _____
Normal coolant temperature range = _____

| Thermostat Temperature | Normal Operating Temperature |
|---|---|
| 180°F (82°C) | Between 180° and 200°F (82° and 93°C) |
| 195°F (91°C) | Between 195° and 215°F (91° and 102°C) |

_____ **2.** Determine the operating temperature of the engine by as many methods as possible including:

- Dash temperature gauge = _____

- Scan tool (ECT) = _____

- Infrared pyrometer = _____

- Other (specify) _____

_____ **3.** Based on the result of the engine operating temperature measurements, what is the necessary action?

_____

_____

# 44

# Drive Trace Pre-Conditioning

**Meets NATEF Task:** (A8-A-2) Research applicable vehicle and service information, such as engine management system operation, vehicle history, service precautions, and TSBs. (P-1)

---

**Name** _____ **Date** _____ **Time on Task** _____

**Make/Model** _____ **Year** _____ **Evaluation:** 4 3 2 1

_____ **1.** Check service information for the specified drive trace pre-conditioning procedures for the following monitors:

  a. All monitors: _____

  _____

  _____

  b. Oxygen sensor heater monitor: _____

  _____

  c. Oxygen sensor monitor: _____

  _____

  d. Catalytic converter monitor: _____

  _____

  e. Evaporative emission control (EVAP) monitor: _____

  _____

  f. Exhaust gas recirculation (EGR) monitor: _____

  _____

```
             Powertrain

F0: Diagnostic Trouble Codes (DTC)
F1: Data Display
F2: Special Functions
F3: Snapshot
F4: I/M System Information
F5: ID Information
```

```
          I/M System Status

Emission Related DTC(s):
  Number of DTC(s)           3
  MIL Requested            YES

Test                  Completed
Catalyst                    No
EVAP                        No
HO2S/O2S                    No
HO2S Heater                 No
EGR                         No
```

# 45

# OBD II Connector Identification

**Meets NATEF Task:** (A8-A-4) Locate and interpret vehicle and major component
identification information. (P-1)

---

**Name** _Zach, Warren_         **Date** _____         **Time on Task** _____

**Make/Model** _____         **Year** _____         **Evaluation:** 4  3  2  1

✓ **1.** Check service information and check which cavities of the OBD II diagnostic link
connector (DLC) have electrical (metal) terminals.

✓ **2.** Use service information and determine the identification for each of the terminals.

1. _Sw-LS-CAN_
2. _N/A_
3. _MS-CAN_
4. _Chassis ground_
5. _Signal Ground_
6. _ISO HS-CAN_
7. _N/A_
8. _N/A_
9. _Dw-FT-CAN_
10. _N/C_
11. _MS-CAN_
12. _K-Line_
13. _Reserved_
14. _ISO HS-CAN_
15. _N/A_
16. _Battery +_

**OBD II Diagnostic Connector**

Pin 1  = Discretionary
Pin 2  = Communication Bus (+)
Pin 3  = Discretionary
Pin 4  = Chassis Ground
Pin 5  = Signal Ground
Pin 6  = Discretionary
Pin 7  = ISO K Line
Pin 8  = Discretionary
Pin 9  = Discretionary
Pin 10 = Communications Bus (-)
Pin 11 = Discretionary
Pin 12 = Discretionary
Pin 13 = Discretionary
Pin 14 = Discretionary
Pin 15 = ISO L Line
Pin 16 = Battery

N/A
N/A
MS-CAN
NIC
MS-CAN
K-Line
Reserved
ISO HS-CAN
N/A
Battery +

# 46

# Retrieving OBD II Diagnostic Trouble Codes

**Meets NATEF Task:** (A8-B-2) Diagnose the causes of emissions or driveability concerns resulting from malfunctions in the computerized engine control system with stored diagnostic trouble codes. (P-1)

---

**Name** _Zach, Warren_     **Date** _____     **Time on Task** _____

**Make/Model** _____     **Year** _____     **Evaluation:** 4   3   2   1

A scan tool is required to retrieve diagnostic trouble codes from an OBD II vehicle. Every OBD II scan tool will be able to read all generic **Society of Automotive Engineers (SAE)** DTCs from any vehicle.

_____ **1.** Retrieve the DTCs using a scan tool.

      (Specify which scan tool was used = _Snap on_.) _Verus_

      _____ _____ _____ _____ _____

_____ **2.** If no DTCs are displayed, set a DTC by disconnecting a sensor such as the throttle position (TP) sensor and then starting and running the engine.

_____ **3.** Did the scan tool display both a generic OBD II (Poxxx) code *and* a manufacturer's specific DTC (P1xxx) code?

      **Yes** _____    **No** _✓_

_____ **4.** Clear the stored DTCs using the scan tool.

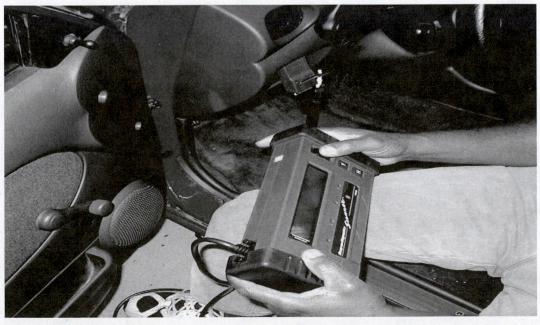

# Set Opposite Code

**Meets NATEF Task:** (A8-B-2) Diagnose the causes of emissions or driveability concerns resulting from malfunctions in the computerized engine control system with stored diagnostic trouble codes. (P-1)

---

**Name** Zach, Warren      **Date** _____     **Time on Task** _____

**Make/Model** _____     **Year** _____     **Evaluation:** 4   3   2   1

If a diagnostic trouble code is set, a commonly used method of diagnosis is to attempt to set the opposite code after clearing the original code. For example, if a throttle position (TP) code is set, clear the DTC and attempt to set a DTC for the opposite condition.

- If a signal high DTC is set, clear the code and turn the ignition switch on (engine off), unplug the sensor and a signal low DTC should be set.

- If a signal low DTC is set, unplug the sensor connector and using a jumper wire, connect the 5-volt reference to the signal terminal in the connector (not at the sensor). Turn the ignition switch on (engine off) and the opposite DTC should set.

✓ **1.** Set a DTC for TP or MAP sensor.

        a. Which sensor was used? TP

        b. What code set? P0122

        c. Meaning of code set? TP Sensor 1 Circuit Low Voltage

✓ **2.** Clear the DTC.

✓ **3.** Disconnect the sensor wiring and use a jumper wire to set the opposite code.

        a. What code was set? P0223

        b. OK ✓    NOT OK _____

**Results:**

If the opposite code *does* set, the cause of the original DTC is the result of a fault in the sensor (component) itself.

If the opposite DTC *does not* set, the problem is likely due to a wiring fault.

> **NOTE:** Always consult a factory service manual for the factors that must be met for a DTC to be set. Be sure that all factors are present when attempting to set the opposite code.

# Freeze Frame and MIL Activity

**Meets NATEF Task:** (A8-B-2) Diagnose the causes of emissions or driveability concerns resulting from malfunctions in the computerized engine control system with stored DTCs. (P-1)

Name _____ Date _____ Time on Task _____

Make/Model _____ Year _____ Evaluation: 4 3 2 1

The purpose of this activity is to allow the service technician apply the use of freeze frames in the diagnosis of OBD II faults.

_____ 1. Connect a scan tool with the key on, engine off (KOEO), and disconnect the electrical connection from the throttle position (TP) sensor. Wait 3 seconds.

_____ 2. A TP sensor TP fault diagnostic trouble code (DTC) should have been set.

_____ Yes (DTC was set)     _____ No (no DTC was set) Turn the ignition off and back on. Did the DTC set?
_____ Yes _____ No

_____ 3. Using a scan tool, view the freeze frame created when the DTC was set.

_____ OK (freeze frame was set) _____ No (freeze frame was not set)

_____ 4. Is the malfunction indicator lamp (MIL or check engine) on? _____ Yes _____ No

_____ 5. Check service information and list the reason(s) that could cause the MIL to be on in the event of a disconnected TP sensor.

_____

_____

_____ 6. Check service information and determine what needs to occur to turn off the MIL.

_____

_____

DLC CONNECTOR

SCAN TOOL CONNECTED TO THE DLC

| 1 | 2 | 3 | 4 | 5 | 6 | 7 | 8 |
|---|---|---|---|---|---|---|---|
| 9 | 10 | 11 | 12 | 13 | 14 | 15 | 16 |

16 PIN OBD II
DATA LINK CONNECTOR
(DLC)

# 49

# No-Code Diagnosis of Driveability Concerns

**Meets NATEF Task:** (A8-B-6) Diagnose the causes of driveability concerns resulting from malfunctions in the computerized engine control system with no stored diagnostic trouble codes. (P-1)

Name _____ Date _____ Time on Task _____

Make/Model _____ Year _____ Evaluation:  4  3  2  1

_____ 1. Check service information for the specified procedures that should be followed when diagnosing a driveability-related concern without any stored diagnostic trouble codes.

_____

_____

_____

_____ 2. Which driveability concerns are being diagnosed? (Check all that apply.)

_____ Hesitation during acceleration
_____ Rough or unstable idle
_____ Stalling
_____ Missing
_____ Other (describe) _____

_____ 3. Based on the results of the scan tool diagnosis, what is the necessary action?

_____

_____

_____

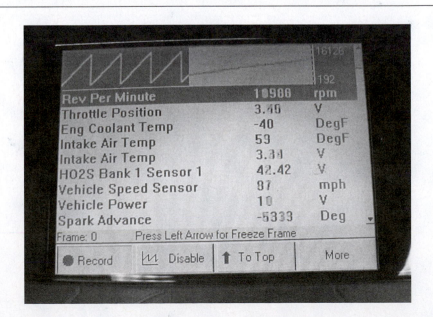

# 50

# Misfire Monitor Activity

**Meets NATEF Task:** (A8-B-7) Obtain and interpret scan tool data. (P-1)

**Name** Zach, Warren     **Date** _____    **Time on Task** _____

**Make/Model** _____    **Year** _____    **Evaluation:** 4  3  2  1

✓ 1. Check service information for the details regarding how the misfire monitor reacts to a misfire and under what engine operating conditions.

_____

_____

HO2S Data

Misfire Data

EVAP Data

✓ 2. Connect a scan tool to the data link connector (DLC) and create a misfire. (Use a spark tester connected to one removed spark plug wire to create an ignition misfire without doing any harm to the vehicle.)

✓ 3. Observe the misfire monitor on the scan tool and record. _____

_____

✓ 4. Rapidly depress the accelerator pedal to wide-open throttle (WOT) a few times. Did the misfire monitor change?

   ✓ Yes   ___ No  Explain: _____

_____

✓ 5. Turn the ignition key off, and then back on.  Did a misfire diagnostic trouble code (DTC) set?

   ___ Yes   ✓ No

✓ 6. Check freeze frame information on the scan tool.  Was freeze frame stored?

   ✓ Yes   ___ No  Why? _____

✓ 7. Based on this activity, what action is necessary? nothing _____

_____

# 51

# Module Identification and Status

**Meets NATEF Task:** (A8-B-4) Check for module communication (including CAN/BUS systems) errors using a scan tool. (P-2)

Name _____ Date _____ Time on Task _____

Make/Model _____ Year _____ Evaluation: 4  3  2  1

_____ 1. Check service information for the procedure and scan tool configuration needed to identify the modules that are on the vehicle network.

_____

_____

_____

_____

```
   MODULE STATUS
ECU              DTC(S)
($10) PCM/VCM      NO
($28) ABS/TCS      NO
($40) BCM/DIM      NO



[ENTER] Review DTCs
```

_____ 2. Using the specified scan tool and procedures, determine the modules that are on the vehicle being tested.

| Module Name | Purpose of Module |
|---|---|
| _____ | _____ |
| _____ | _____ |
| _____ | _____ |
| _____ | _____ |
| _____ | _____ |
| _____ | _____ |

_____ 3. What is the status of the modules? _____

_____

_____ 4. Are there any modules missing from the scan tool display that are known to be on the vehicle?

_____ Yes _____ No (describe) _____

# 52

# Temperature Sensor Visual Inspection

**Meets NATEF Task:** (A8-B-5) Inspect and test sensors, actuators, and circuits using a graphing multimeter (GMM)/digital storage oscilloscope (DSO); perform necessary action. (P-1)

**Name** _Zach Bentley_          **Date** _____     **Time on Task** _____

**Make/Model** _____     **Year** _____     **Evaluation:** 4  3  2  1

_____ 1. Check service information for the location, wire colors, and specified testing procedures for the temperature sensor.

Location: _Under radiator hose_

Wire colors and purpose: _Blue, red_

_____

Recommended testing procedure: _-40°F, 278°F_

_____

_____ 2. Describe the actual location of the temperature sensor. _under radiator hose_

_____ 3. Verify the wire colors and the location in the electrical connector.

OK _✓_   NOT OK _____   Describe fault: _____

_____

_____ 4. Check the condition of the electrical terminals.

OK _✓_   NOT OK _____   Describe fault: _____

_____

_____ 5. Check the physical condition of the sensor for signs of contamination or damage.

OK _✓_   NOT OK _____   Describe fault: _____

_____

_____ 6. Based on the inspection, what is the necessary action? _It's okay_

_____

# ECT Sensor DMM Testing

**Meets NATEF Task:** (A8-B-5) Inspect and test sensors, actuators, and circuits using a graphing multimeter (GMM)/digital storage oscilloscope (DSO); perform necessary action. (P-1)

**Name** Zach Bentley      **Date** _____      **Time on Task** _____

**Make/Model** _____      **Year** _____      **Evaluation:** 4   3   2   1

✓ **1.** Check service information for the specified voltage and/or resistance specifications and testing procedures.

Voltage/resistance specifications: -40°F = 100,700 Ω,

70°F = 3,077 Ω

Specified testing procedures: _____

_____

✓ **2.** List the steps performed and the test results obtained.

_____

_____

_____

_____

**3.** Do the sensor test results match the specifications?

✓ Yes   ____ No (explain why not) _____

_____

_____

✓ **4.** Based on the test results, what is the necessary action? Nothing

_____

_____

$0.8\% = 1.00, 100 - \Omega$

69

16°C   27°C

N=k

[I+k of 3]

# 54

We Support NATEF

# Temperature Sensors

**Meets NATEF Task:** (A8-B-5) Inspect and test sensors, actuators, and circuits using a graphing multimeter (GMM)/digital storage oscilloscope (DSO); perform necessary action. (P-1)

---

**Name** _Zach Bentley_    **Date** _____    **Time on Task** _____

**Make/Model** _____    **Year** _____    **Evaluation:  4   3   2   1**

✓____ **1.** Locate the engine coolant temperature (ECT) sensor used by the engine computer.

Wire colors = _Blue_ and _Red_ .

_____ **2.** Locate and identify these coolant temperature sensors and list their *wire color(s)* in the blanks below:

     a.  sensor for dash "hot" *light* = _____.

     b.  sensor for dash temperature *gauge* = _____.

     c.  sensor for electric cooling fan = _____.

     d.  sensor for cold start injector on some fuel injected engines _____.

     e.  sensor for intake air temperature (IAT) = _____.
        (may be located in the air cleaner)

✓____ **3.** Based on the test results, what is the necessary action?

_____

_____

_____

# 55

# Engine Coolant Temperature (ECT) Graph

**Meets NATEF Task:** (A8-B-5) Inspect and test sensors, actuators, and circuits using a graphing multimeter (GMM)/digital storage oscilloscope (DSO); perform necessary action. (P-1)

Name _Zach Bentley_     Date _____     Time on Task _____

Make/Model _____     Year _____     Evaluation: 4   3   2   1

Most engine coolant temperature sensors (ECTs) use a negative temperature coefficient (NCT) thermistor. The resistance of the sensor decreases as the temperature of the engine coolant increases. The vehicle computer applies a voltage to the sensor. The purpose of this worksheet is to plot the relationship of the ECT sensor temperature and the voltage.

_____ 1. Carefully back probe the signal wire of the engine coolant temperature (ECT) sensor.

_____ 2. Set the digital multimeter to read DC volts.

_____ 3. Connect a scan tool or use a pyrometer to measure engine coolant temperature.

_____ 4. Plot the voltage of the ECT every 10° as the engine warms up.

> **NOTE:** Many engine computers connect another resistor in the ECT circuit when the temperature of the coolant reaches 120°-140°. This causes the voltage at the ECT sensor to rise, then continue to fall as the coolant temperature continues to rise.

**TEMPERATURE (°F)**

_____ 5. Was there a upward movement of the graph when the thermostat opened?

     YES _____     NO _✓_

_____ 6. Was there a slight movement upward when the cooling fan came on?

     YES _____     NO _✓_

_____ 7. Based on the test results, what is the necessary action? _____

# 56

# Temperature Sensor Scan Tool Diagnosis

**Meets NATEF Task:** (A8-B-5) Inspect and test sensors, actuators, and circuits using a graphing multimeter (GMM)/digital storage oscilloscope (DSO); perform necessary action. (P-1)

Name _Zach Bentley_  Date _____  Time on Task _____

Make/Model _____  Year _____  Evaluation:  4  3  2  1

_____ 1. Check service information for the recommended method for checking temperature sensors using a scan tool.

_____

_____

_____ 2. List all of the temperature sensors that are on the vehicle. Check all that apply.

_____ ECT (describe location) _____

_____ IAT (describe location) _____

_____ TFT (describe location) _____

_____ Other (describe) _____

_____ 3. On a vehicle that has not been operated for several hours, use a scan tool and list the temperature displayed for various temperature sensors.

ECT = _____

IAT = _____

TFT = _____

Other (describe) = _____

_____

_____ 4. Based on the test results, what is the necessary action? _____

_____

# 57

We Support
NATEF

# Throttle Position Sensor Visual Inspection

**Meets NATEF Task:** (A8-B-5) Inspect and test sensors, actuators, and circuits using a graphing multimeter (GMM)/digital storage oscilloscope (DSO); perform necessary action. (P-1)

Name _____ Date _____ Time on Task _____

Make/Model _____ Year _____ Evaluation: 4  3  2  1

_____ 1. Check service information for the location, wire colors, and specified testing procedures for the throttle position sensor.

Throttle Sensor

Location: _____

Wire colors and purpose: _____

_____

Recommended testing procedure: _____

_____

_____ 2. Describe the actual location of the throttle position sensor. _____

_____ 3. Verify the wire colors and the location in the electrical connector.

**OK** ____ **NOT OK** ____ Describe fault: _____

_____

_____ 4. Check the condition of the electrical terminals.

**OK** ____ **NOT OK** ____ Describe fault: _____

_____

_____ 5. Check the physical condition of the sensor for signs of contamination or damage.

**OK** ____ **NOT OK** ____ Describe fault: _____

_____

_____ 6. Based on the inspection, what is the necessary action? _____

_____

# 58

# Throttle Position Sensor DMM Testing

**Meets NATEF Task:** (A8-B-5) Inspect and test sensors, actuators, and circuits using a graphing multimeter (GMM)/digital storage oscilloscope (DSO); perform necessary action. (P-1)

**Name** Zach Bentley     **Date** _____     **Time on Task** _____

**Make/Model** _____     **Year** _____     **Evaluation:  4  3  2  1**

_____ 1. Check service information for the specified voltage and/or resistance specifications and testing procedures.

     Voltage/resistance specifications: _____

     _____

     Specified testing procedures: _____

     _____

_____ 2. List the steps performed and the test results obtained.

     _____

     _____

     _____

     _____

— 5 volts
— Sensor Output
— Ground

**Throttle Position Sensor**

_____ 3. Do the sensor test results match the specifications?

     ____ Yes    ____ No (explain why not) _____

     _____

     _____

_____ 4. Based on the test results, what is the necessary action? _____

     _____

     _____

# 59

We Support NATEF

# Throttle Position Sensor Scope Test

**Meets NATEF Task:** (A8-B-5) Inspect and test sensors, actuators, and circuits using a graphing multimeter (GMM)/digital storage oscilloscope (DSO); perform necessary action. (P-1)

**Name** Zach Bentley          **Date** _____     **Time on Task** _____

**Make/Model** _____     **Year** _____     **Evaluation:** 4  3  2  1

_____ **1.** Check service information regarding the location of the throttle position sensor used on the vehicle being tested.

Location (describe):

by air cleaner

_____ **2.** Check service information for the wire colors used and their purpose

Wire 1 (color and purpose):          _____

Wire 2 (color and purpose):          _____

Wire 3 (color and purpose):          _____

_____ **3.** Check service information for the specified voltage output and/or waveform for the throttle position sensor.

          _____

_____ **4.** Following the test equipment manufacturer's instructions, show the instructor the waveform.

          Instructor OK _____✓_____

_____ **5.** Based on the comparison between the captured waveform and the specified waveform, what action is needed?

          Nothing

          _____

# 60

We Support
NATEF

# TP Sensor Voltmeter Test

**Meets NATEF Task:** (A8-B-5) Inspect and test sensors, actuators, and circuits using a graphing multimeter (GMM)/digital storage oscilloscope (DSO); perform necessary action. (P-1)

Name _Zach. Bentley_     Date _____    Time on Task _____

Make/Model _____    Year _____    Evaluation:  4  3  2  1

_____ 1. Check service information for the location, specifications for the throttle position (TP) sensor.

_____ 2. Carefully backprobe the wires at the connector to gain access to the 5-volt reference, signal, and signal return (ground) terminal.

_____ 3. With the ignition on, engine off (KOEO), set the digital multimeter (DMM) to DC volts and attach the black meter lead to a good clean engine ground.

_____ 4. Measure the reference voltage (should be close to 5 volts) = _5.04_ .

_____ 5. Measure the sensor signal voltage at idle _3.9_ ,

       specification = _____ .

_____ 6. Measure the TP sensor at wide-open throttle (W.O.T.) = _____ volts (should be about 4.5 volts).

_____ 7. Measure the voltage (voltage drop) between the signal return at the TP sensor and a good clean engine ground.

       _____ volts (should be less than 0.2 volts)

_____ 8. Based on the test results, what is the necessary action?

_____

_____

_____

Throttle Sensor

# 61

We Support
NATEF

# TP Graph Test

**Meets NATEF Task:** (A8-B-5) Inspect and test sensors, actuators, and circuits using a graphing multimeter (GMM)/digital storage oscilloscope (DSO); perform necessary action. (P-1)

**Name** Zach Bentley          **Date** _____          **Time on Task** _____

**Make/Model** _____          **Year** _____          **Evaluation:  4   3   2   1**

The engine computer supplies a 5 volt reference voltage to the variable resistance throttle position sensor. At idle, the throttle position voltage as measured by the output of the TP sensor should be about 0.5 volt and about 4.5 volts when the throttle is in the wide open position.

_____  1.  Carefully back probe the signal terminal of the TP sensor using a T-pin.

_____  2.  Connect the red lead of a digital meter set to read DC volts to the T-pin and the black lead to a good chassis ground.

_____  3.  Turn the ignition switch to on (engine off) and record the TP voltage at idle, ¼ throttle, ½ throttle, ¾ throttle and wide open throttle (WOT).

| | | | | |
|---|---|---|---|---|
| | | | | |
| | | | | |
| | | | | |
| | | | | |

**Idle          ¼          ½          ¾          WOT**

_____  4.  Place a dot at each point on the graph at idle, ¼, ½, ¾, and WOT. Connect the dots. The results should be a straight line.

  **OK** _____     **NOT OK** _____

_____  5.  Based on the test results, what is the necessary action? _____

_____

_____

# 62

# Throttle Position Sensor Scan Tool Diagnosis

**Meets NATEF Task:** (A8-B-5) Inspect and test sensors, actuators, and circuits using a graphing multimeter (GMM)/digital storage oscilloscope (DSO); perform necessary action. (P-1)

**Name** Zach Bentley          **Date** _____   **Time on Task** _____

**Make/Model** _____   **Year** _____   **Evaluation:** 4  3  2  1

_____ 1. Check service information for the specified testing procedures and specifications for the throttle position (TP) sensor.

   Recommended testing procedure: _____

   Throttle position sensor specification: _____

_____ 2. Connect a scan tool to the data link connector (DLC). Check and record any throttle position-related diagnostic trouble codes (DTCs).

| DTC | Description of DTC |
|-----|--------------------|
| _____ | _____ |
| _____ | _____ |
| _____ | _____ |

_____ 3. With the ignition on, engine off (KOEO), connect a scan tool and check the output of the TP sensor at:

   Idle = _____   ½ throttle = _____   Wide open (WOT) = _____

_____ 4. Based on the test results, what is the necessary action?

   _____

   _____

   _____

   _____

# 63

We Support **NATEF**

# MAP Sensor Visual Inspection

**Meets NATEF Task:** (A8-B-5) Inspect and test sensors, actuators, and circuits using a graphing multimeter (GMM)/digital storage oscilloscope (DSO); perform necessary action. (P-1)

Name _____ Date _____ Time on Task _____

Make/Model _____ Year _____ Evaluation: 4 3 2 1

_____ 1. Check service information for the location, wire colors, and specified testing procedures for the MAP sensor.

Location: _____

Wire colors and purpose: _____

_____

Recommended testing procedure: _____

_____

_____ 2. Describe the actual location of the MAP sensor. _____

_____ 3. Verify the wire colors and the location in the electrical connector.

**OK** ____ **NOT OK** ____ Describe fault: _____

_____

_____ 4. Check the condition of the electrical terminals.

**OK** ____ **NOT OK** ____ Describe fault: _____

_____

_____ 5. Check the physical condition of the sensor for signs of contamination or damage.

**OK** ____ **NOT OK** ____ Describe fault: _____

_____

_____ 6. Based on the inspection, what is the necessary action? _____

_____

# 64

# MAP Sensor DMM Testing

**Meets NATEF Task:** (A8-B-5) Inspect and test sensors, actuators, and circuits using a graphing multimeter (GMM)/digital storage oscilloscope (DSO); perform necessary action. (P-1)

Name _____ Date _____ Time on Task _____

Make/Model _____ Year _____ Evaluation: 4  3  2  1

_____ 1. Check service information for the specified voltage and/or resistance specifications and testing procedures.

       Voltage/resistance specifications: _____

       _____

       Specified testing procedures: _____

       _____

_____ 2. List the steps performed and the test results obtained.

       _____

       _____

       _____

       _____

_____ 3. Do the sensor test results match the specifications?

       ____ Yes  ____ No (explain why not) _____

       _____

       _____

_____ 4. Based on the test results, what is the necessary action? _____

       _____

# 65

# MAP Sensor Waveform Test

**Meets NATEF Task:** (A8-B-5) Inspect and test sensors, actuators, and circuits using a graphing multimeter (GMM)/digital storage oscilloscope (DSO); perform necessary action. (P-1)

Name _____   Date _____   Time on Task _____

Make/Model _____   Year _____   Evaluation:  4  3  2  1

_____ 1. Check service information regarding the location of the MAP sensor used on the vehicle being tested.

Location (describe): _____

_____ 2. Check service information for the wire colors used and their purpose.

Wire 1 (color and purpose): _____

Wire 2 (color and purpose): _____

Wire 3 (color and purpose): _____

```
[▼][□][⊘] ×|10 ms/div ▼| |×2 ▼| A|6      ▼| |DC ▼||Off ▼| B|Off       ▼| |AC ▼||Off ▼|

6.0
5.4
4.8
4.2
3.6
3.0
2.4
1.8
1.2
0.6
0.0
    0    5    10   15   20   25   30   35   40   45   50
                                                        ms
       ch A: Frequency (Hz)              109.2
            MAP Sensor (Digital)
```

_____ 3. Check service information for the specified voltage output and/or waveform for the MAP sensor.

_____

_____ 4. Following the test equipment manufacturer's instructions, show the instructor the waveforms.                        Instructor OK _____

_____ 5. Based on the comparison between the captured waveform and the specified waveform, what action is needed?

_____

# 66

# MAP Sensor Diagnosis

**Meets NATEF Task:** (A8-B-5) Inspect and test sensors, actuators, and circuits using a graphing multimeter (GMM)/digital storage oscilloscope (DSO); perform necessary action. (P-1)

Name _____ Date _____ Time on Task _____

Make/Model _____ Year _____ Evaluation: 4 3 2 1

_____ 1. Check service information for the specified MAP sensor diagnosis procedure.

_____

_____ 2. Perform a thorough visual inspection including:

    a. Check the condition of vacuum hose (if equipped).
    b. Check that the vacuum hose routing does not have any dips or sags in the vacuum hose between the sensor and the intake manifold.

> **NOTE:** A dip or low portion in the vacuum hose can create a trap where liquid fuel (condensed gasoline fumes) or water (condensed steam) can accumulate and block the vacuum signal to the MAP sensor.

    c. Disconnect the vacuum hose (if equipped) from the MAP sensor. If anything such as a liquid or other substance comes out of the sensor or the hose, replace the MAP sensor. Reconnect the vacuum hose to the MAP.

_____ 3. Turn the ignition key on (engine off), read and record the MAP sensor voltage (or frequency) = _____ volts (Hz) (use either a scan tool or digital meter connected to the signal wire). (Should be about 4.60 to 4.80 volts or 156-159 Hz.)

    **OK _____ NOT OK _____**

_____ 4. Start the engine and operate until normal operating temperature is achieved. Read and record the MAP sensor voltage (or Hz) at idle speed = _____volts (Hz). (Should be between 0.9 and 1.6 volts (102-109 Hz) if the engine varies between 17 and 21 inches of Hg.) **OK _____ NOT OK _____**

_____ 5. Using a GMM or DSO, graph the output signal from the MAP sensor and compare it (draw the pattern displayed).

_____ 6. Based on these tests, what is the necessary action? _____

_____

# 67

# MAP Sensor Output Chart

**Meets NATEF Task:** (A8-B-5) Inspect and test sensors, actuators, and circuits using a graphing multimeter (GMM)/digital storage oscilloscope (DSO); perform necessary action. (P-1)

Name _____ Date _____ Time on Task _____

Make/Model _____ Year _____ Evaluation: 4 3 2 1

Most vehicle MAP sensors use a 5-volt reference, a signal return and a ground connection. As the vacuum inside the intake manifold changes, the MAP sensor voltage changes.

- High vacuum (low absolute manifold pressure) = low voltage
- Low vacuum (high absolute manifold pressure) = high voltage

_____ 1. Connect a T-pin to the signal wire connector at the MAP sensor.

_____ 2. Connect the red lead of a digital voltmeter set to read DC volts to the T-pin. Connect the black meter lead to a good chassis ground.

_____ 3. Disconnect the vacuum hose from the MAP sensor (or remove the sensor from the manifold) and attach a hand-operated vacuum pump to the sensor.

_____ 4. Place a dot on the graph that represents the MAP sensor voltage when 5, 10, 15, 20, 25 and 30 in. Hg of vacuum is applied to the sensor.

_____ 5. Connect the dots. The results should be a straight line.

OK _____    NOT OK _____

```
       0        5        10        15        20        25        30
                        VACUUM APPLIED (in. Hg)
```

_____ 6. Based on the results of this test, what is the necessary action? _____

_____

# 68

# MAF Sensor Visual Inspection

**Meets NATEF Task:** (A8-B-5) Inspect and test sensors, actuators, and circuits using a graphing multimeter (GMM)/digital storage oscilloscope (DSO); perform necessary action. (P-1)

Name _____ Date _____ Time on Task _____

Make/Model _____ Year _____ Evaluation: 4 3 2 1

_____ 1. Check service information for the location, wire colors, and specified testing procedures for the MAF sensor.

Location: _____

Wire colors and purpose: _____

_____

Recommended testing procedure: _____

_____

_____ 2. Describe the actual location of the MAF sensor. _____

_____ 3. Verify the wire colors and the location in the electrical connector.

**OK** ____ **NOT OK** ____ Describe fault: _____

_____

_____ 4. Check the condition of the electrical terminals.

**OK** ____ **NOT OK** ____ Describe fault: _____

_____

_____ 5. Check the physical condition of the sensor for signs of contamination or damage.

**OK** ____ **NOT OK** ____ Describe fault: _____

_____

_____ 6. Based on the inspection, what is the necessary action? _____

_____

# 69

# Air Vane Sensor DMM Testing

**Meets NATEF Task:** (A8-B-5) Inspect and test sensors, actuators, and circuits using a graphing multimeter (GMM)/digital storage oscilloscope (DSO); perform necessary action. (P-1)

Name _____ Date _____ Time on Task _____

Make/Model _____ Year _____ Evaluation: 4   3   2   1

_____ 1. Check service information for the specified voltage and/or resistance specifications and testing procedures.

Voltage/resistance specifications: _____

_____

Specified testing procedures: _____

_____

_____ 2. List the steps performed and the test results obtained.

_____

_____

_____

_____

_____ 3. Do the sensor test results match the specifications?

_____ Yes   _____ No (explain why not)

_____

_____

_____

_____ 4. Based on the test results, what is the necessary action?

_____

_____

# 70

# Air Vane Sensor Waveform Testing

**Meets NATEF Task:** (A8-B-5) Inspect and test sensors, actuators, and circuits using a graphing multimeter (GMM)/digital storage oscilloscope (DSO); perform necessary action. (P-1)

Name _____   Date _____   Time on Task _____

Make/Model _____   Year _____   Evaluation:  4  3  2  1

_____ 1. Check service information regarding the location of the MAF sensor used on the vehicle being tested.

Location (describe): _____

_____ 2. Check service information for the wire colors used and their purpose.

Wire 1 (color and purpose): _____

Wire 2 (color and purpose): _____

Wire 3 (color and purpose): _____

_____ 3. Check service information for the specified voltage output and/or waveform for the MAF sensor.

_____

Check which: ___ digital
___ analog

_____ 4. Following the test equipment manufacturer's instructions, show the instructor the waveforms.                     Instructor OK _____

_____ 5. Based on the comparison between the captured waveform and the specified waveform, what action is needed?

_____

# 71

# MAF Sensor Diagnosis

**Meets NATEF Task:** (A8-B-5) Inspect and test sensors, actuators, and circuits using a graphing multimeter (GMM)/digital storage oscilloscope (DSO); perform necessary action. (P-1)

Name _____   Date _____   Time on Task _____

Make/Model _____   Year _____   Evaluation: 4  3  2  1

A "*Mass Air Flow*" sensor produces a variable output depending on the MASS of the air flow through the sensor. A faulty MAF can cause driveability problems and stalling. A good MAF sensor should produce a signal that increases with engine speed.

_____ 1. Check service information for the specified procedure to follow to test the MAF sensor.

_____

_____ 2. Use a meter or scope with a frequency counter to record frequency or voltage at idle and at WOT (short bursts).

at idle = _____      at WOT = _____

_____ 3. Use a scan tool and record grams per second.

at idle = _____      at WOT = _____

A good MAF should read:

- greater than 100 grams per second (scan tool diagnosis)
- higher than 7000 Hertz (7 KHz) (digital MAF)
- higher than 4 volts (analog MAF)

_____ 4. If the MAF sensor reading does not exceed these values, the sensing wire may be contaminated or the sensor itself is defective.

_____ 5. Based on the test results, what is the necessary action? _____

_____

_____

# 72

We Support
NATEF

# MAF Sensor Scope

**Meets NATEF Task:** (A8-B-5) Inspect and test sensors, actuators, and circuits using a graphing multimeter (GMM)/digital storage oscilloscope (DSO); perform necessary action. (P-1)

---

**Name** _____ **Date** _____ **Time on Task** _____

**Make/Model** _____ **Year** _____ **Evaluation:** 4  3  2  1

Most mass air flow sensors produce a variable frequency signal or voltage proportional to the amount (mass) of air flowing through the sensor.

_____ **1.** Check service information and determine the voltage (analog MAF sensor) or frequency (digital MAF sensor) range for the unit on the vehicle being tested.

_____

_____ **2.** Set the scope to 2ms/div and 200 mV/div.

_____ **3.** Locate the MAF sensor and connect the scope probe to the signal wire on the sensor by carefully back probing the connector.

_____ **3.** Connect the scope probe ground lead to a good non-painted engine or body ground.

_____ **4.** Draw the MAF sensor signal at idle speed with the engine in neutral or park.

<br><br><br><br><br><br>

_____ **5.** Place the gear selector in drive or reverse (automatic transmissions only) and draw the MAF sensor signal.

<br><br><br><br><br>

_____ **6.** What difference did you notice? _____

_____

_____ **7.** Based on the test results, what is the necessary action? _____

# 73

# Oxygen Sensor Visual Inspection

**Meets NATEF Task:** (A8-B-5) Inspect and test sensors, actuators, and circuits using a graphing multimeter (GMM)/digital storage oscilloscope (DSO); perform necessary action. (P-1)

**Name** _Zach Warren_ **Date** _____ **Time on Task** _____

**Make/Model** _____ **Year** _____ **Evaluation:** 4 3 2 1

✓ 1. Check service information for the location, wire colors, and specified testing procedures for the oxygen sensor.

    Location: _____

    Wire colors and purpose: _____

    _____

    Recommended testing procedure: _____

    _____

✓ 2. Describe the actual location of the oxygen sensor. _behind cat_

✓ 3. Verify the wire colors and the location in the electrical connector.

    OK ✓ NOT OK ____ Describe fault: _____

    _____

✓ 4. Check the condition of the electrical terminals.

    OK ____ NOT OK ____ Describe fault: _____

    _____

✓ 5. Check the physical condition of the sensor for signs of contamination or damage.

    OK ✓ NOT OK ____ Describe fault: _____

    _____

✓ 6. Based on the inspection, what is the necessary action? _Nothing_

    _____

# 74

# Oxygen Sensor DMM Testing

**Meets NATEF Task:** (A8-B-5) Inspect and test sensors, actuators, and circuits using a graphing multimeter (GMM)/digital storage oscilloscope (DSO); perform necessary action. (P-1)

**Name** Zach, Warren    **Date** _____    **Time on Task** _____

**Make/Model** _____    **Year** _____    **Evaluation:** 4 3 2 1

1. Check service information for the specified voltage and/or resistance specifications and testing procedures.

   Voltage/resistance specifications: _____

   _____

   Specified testing procedures: _____

   _____

2. List the steps performed and the test results obtained.

   _____

   _____

   _____

   _____

   OHMS

   Oxygen Sensor Heater Resistance Test

3. Do the sensor test results match the specifications?

   __ Yes __ No (explain why not) _____

   _____

   _____

4. Based on the test results, what is the necessary action? Nothing

   _____

# 75

# Wide-Band Oxygen Sensor

**Meets NATEF Task:** (A8-B-5) Inspect and test sensors, actuators, and circuits using a graphing multimeter (GMM)/digital storage oscilloscope (DSO); perform necessary action. (P-1)

Name _____ Date _____ Time on Task _____

Make/Model _____ Year _____ Evaluation:  4  3  2  1

_____ 1. Wide-band oxygen sensors use four, five, or six wires. Check service information for the color and identification of each of the wires used on the wide-band oxygen sensors.

| Wire Color | Purpose | Typical Voltage on Wire During Closed-Loop Operation |
|---|---|---|
| a. | | |
| b. | | |
| c. | | |
| d. | | |
| e. | | |
| f. | | |

_____ 2. Check service information for the specified testing procedure for diagnosing the wide-band oxygen sensor.

_____

_____

Check all that are specified:

_____ Scan tool
_____ DMM
_____ DSO
_____ Other (describe) _____

_____ 3. Based on the results of the specified test procedure, what is the necessary action?

_____

# 76

# Oxygen Sensor Waveform Testing

**Meets NATEF Task:** (A8-B-5) Inspect and test sensors, actuators, and circuits using a graphing multimeter (GMM)/digital storage oscilloscope (DSO); perform necessary action. (P-1)

Name _Zach, Warren_     Date _____     Time on Task _____

Make/Model _____     Year _____     Evaluation:  4  3  2  1

✓ 1. Check service information regarding the location of the oxygen sensor used on the vehicle being tested.

     Location (describe): _behind cat_

✓ 2. Check service information for the wire colors used and their purpose.

     Wire 1 (color and purpose): _Tan + wht / signal_
     Wire 2 (color and purpose): _Pur + wht_
     Wire 3 (color and purpose): _____

✓ 3. Check service information for the specified voltage output and/or waveform for the oxygen sensor.

     _____

✓ 4. Following the test equipment manufacturer's instructions, show the instructor the waveforms.

       Instructor OK _____

✓ 5. Based on the comparison between the captured waveform and the specified waveform, what action is needed?

     _nothing_ _____

     _____

| 800 mV MAXIMUM | HOLD |
| 0.00 V MINIMUM | |

1200mV
1000
800
600
400
200
.0            200ms/DIV
RECALL
BACK    ◁ SEARCH ▷    PRINT   SELECT

# 77

# Oxygen Sensor Voltmeter Diagnosis

**Meets NATEF Task:** (A8-B-5) Inspect and test sensors, actuators, and circuits using a graphing multimeter (GMM)/digital storage oscilloscope (DSO); perform necessary action. (P-1)

**Name** Zach, Warren     **Date** _____     **Time on Task** _____

**Make/Model** _____   **Year** _____   **Evaluation: 4 3 2 1**

_____ 1. Locate the oxygen sensor(s) and carefully back probe the sensor wire at a connector with a "T" pin.

_____ 2. Set the digital multimeter to read DC volts (DCV).

_____ 3. Attach the red lead of the digital voltmeter to the sensor and ground the black meter lead to a good clean non-painted ground.

_____ 4. Start the engine and allow it to run at 2500 RPM for 2 minutes to get the oxygen sensor up to operating temperature and get the engine into closed loop.

_____ 5. Select MIN/MAX record and maintain the engine speed at 2500 RPM for 2 additional minutes.

     Record the   MIN _____    MAX _____    AVERAGE _____

_____ 6. Results: MIN should be below 200 mV and MAX should be above 800 mV. The average should be about 450 mV.

     a. If the average is higher than 450 mV, the engine is operating with a rich air-fuel mixture.

     b. If the average is lower than 450 mV, the engine is operating with a lean air-fuel mixture.

_____ 7. Based on the test results, what is the necessary action? nothing _____

_____

# 78

# Oxygen Sensor Scan Tool Diagnosis

**Meets NATEF Task:** (A8-B-5) Inspect and test sensors, actuators, and circuits using a graphing multimeter (GMM)/digital storage oscilloscope (DSO); perform necessary action. (P-1)

Name _Zach, Warren_    Date _____    Time on Task _____

Make/Model _____    Year _____    Evaluation: 4   3   2   1

_____ 1. Connect the scan tool to the DLC and start the engine.

_____ 2. Operate the engine at a fast idle (2500 RPM) for 2 minutes to allow time for the oxygen sensor to warm to operating temperature.

_____ 3. Observe the oxygen sensor activity on the scan tool to verify closed loop operation.

_____ 4. Select "snap shot" mode and hold the engine speed steady and start recording.

_____ 5. Play back snap shot and place a mark beside each range of oxygen sensor voltage for each frame of the snap shot.

**Between 0 and 300 mV**    **Between 300 and 600 mV**    **Between 600 and 1000 mV**

_____    _____    _____
(record # of times)      (record # of times)      (record # of times)

_____ 6. Results: A good oxygen sensor and computer system should result in most snap shot values at both ends (0 to 300 and 600 to 1000 mV). If most of the readings are in the middle, the oxygen sensor is not working correctly.

OK _____    NOT OK _____

_____ 7. Based on the test results, what is the necessary action? _nothing_

_____

# 79

# Oxygen Sensor Scope Diagnosis

**Meets NATEF Task:** (A8-B-5) Inspect and test sensors, actuators, and circuits using a graphing multimeter (GMM)/digital storage oscilloscope (DSO); perform necessary action. (P-1)

**Name** Zach, Warren     **Date** _____    **Time on Task** _____

**Make/Model** _____    **Year** _____    **Evaluation: 4 3 2 1**

✓ _____ **1.** Locate the oxygen sensor(s) and carefully back probe the sensor wire at a connector with a "T" pin.

✓ _____ **2.** Set the scope to 1s/div time base and 200 mV/div for the volts per division setting.

✓ _____ **3.** Attach the scope probe to the oxygen sensor signal wire. Connect the ground wire from the scope probe to a good engine ground.

✓ _____ **4.** Start the engine and allow it to run at 2500 RPM for 2 minutes to allow the oxygen sensor to reach operating temperature and the engine to achieve closed loop operation.

✓ _____ **5.** Select the proper time base and volts per division (try 200 mS per division and 200 mV per division).

✓ _____ **6.** Observe the scope pattern:

     a. What is the highest voltage observed?

     851 mV _____ Max. volts

     b. What is the lowest voltage observed?

     35 mV _____ Min volts

     c. How many times does the voltage cycle in one second? _____
     (Should be 0.5 to 5.0 Hz.)

             **OK** __✓__     **NOT OK** _____

✓ _____ **7.** Based on the results of the test, what is the necessary action? _____

_____

Scope display:

```
800  mV  MAXIMUM        HOLD
0.00  v  MINIMUM

1200mV ·    ·    ·    ·    ·
1000   ·    ·    ·    ·    ·

800
400
200
.0 ·              ·    200ms/DIV
RECALL
   BACK   ⟵ SEARCH ⟶   PRINT  SELECT
```

# 80

# Downstream Oxygen Sensor Diagnosis

**Meets NATEF Task:** (A8-B-5) Inspect and test sensors, actuators, and circuits using a graphing multimeter (GMM)/digital storage oscilloscope (DSO); perform necessary action. (P-1)

**Name** Zach, Warren      **Date** _____    **Time on Task** _____

**Make/Model** _____    **Year** _____    **Evaluation:** 4   3   2   1

____ 1. Check service information for the specified testing and inspection procedures to follow when diagnosing the downstream oxygen sensor.

_____

_____

____ 2. Describe the number and location(s) of the downstream oxygen sensor(s).

behind cat _____

____ 3. Visually check the sensor and wiring for damage or other faults.

____ ✓ **OK** ____ **NOT OK** (describe) _____

____ 4. Test the downstream oxygen sensor using a scan tool and check for normal operation. Describe the test results.

sensor reads well _____

_____

____ 5. Based on the test and the inspection, what is the necessary action? nothing _____

_____

# 81

# Lambda Activity

**Meets NATEF Task:** (A8-B-5) Inspect and test sensors, actuators, and circuits using a graphing multimeter (GMM)/digital storage oscilloscope (DSO); perform necessary action. (P-1)

Name _____ Date _____ Time on Task _____

Make/Model _____ Year _____ Evaluation: 4 3 2 1

_____ 1. Check service information for the specified air-fuel ratio (lambda) for the specific vehicle being tested.

_____

_____

_____ 2. Connect a scan tool and determine the desired or commanded air-fuel ratio (lambda).

_____

_____

_____

_____ 3. Is the commanded or desired air-fuel ratio richer or leaner than stoichiometric?

_____ richer

_____ leaner

_____ 4. Determine the air-fuel ratio for the following lambda numbers:

Leaner than 14.7:1    – lambda $1.221 \times 14.7 =$ _____
                   – lambda $1.101 \times 14.7 =$ _____
Richer than 14.7:1    – lambda $0.989 \times 14.7 =$ _____
                   – lambda $0.890 \times 14.7 =$ _____

_____ 5. Based on the test results, what is the interpretation of the commanded lambda?

_____

_____

# 82

# Wide Band Oxygen Sensor Identification

**Meets NATEF Task:** (None Specified)

Name _____ Date _____ Time on Task _____

Make/Model _____ Year _____ Evaluation:  4  3  2  1

_____ 1. Check service information to determine if the vehicle being serviced is equipped with a wide band oxygen sensor. (check all that apply)

     _____ Visual inspection (5 or more wires from the oxygen sensor)

     _____ Service information

     _____ Scan tool

     _____ Other (describe) _____

_____ 2. What term is used in service information for a wide band oxygen sensor. Check which term is used.

     _____ Wide band oxygen sensor

     _____ Broadband oxygen sensor

     _____ Wide range oxygen sensor

     _____ Air-fuel ratio (AFR) sensor

     _____ Wide range air-fuel (WRAF) sensor

     _____ Lean air-fuel (LAF) sensor

     _____ Air-fuel (AF) sensor

     _____ Other (describe _____

_____ 3. How many wires are there at the sensor end of the electrical connector? _____

_____ 4. How many wires are there at the PCM end of the connector? _____

_____ 5. What is the value of the calibration resistor? _____

# 83

# Fuel Pump Testing

**Meets NATEF Task:** (A8-D-3) Inspect and test fuel pump for pressure, regulation and volume; perform necessary action. (P-1)

Name _____ Date _____ Time on Task _____

Make/Model _____ Year _____ Evaluation: 4 3 2 1

_____ 1. Check service information and determine the factory specifications for acceptable fuel pump pressure.

Fuel pump pressure specifications = _____

_____ 2. Check service information, locate the fuel system pressure test valve or port, and describe its location.

_____

_____ 3. Connect a fuel pressure gauge to the fuel pressure Schrader valve.

_____ 4. Start the engine and observe the fuel pressure.

fuel pressure = _____

OK _____     NOT OK _____

_____ 5. Connect a hand-operated vacuum pump to the fuel pressure regulator and apply 20 in. Hg. of vacuum. Did the pressure decrease? _____

_____ 6. Check fuel pump volume (0.5 to 1.0 gallons per minute).

_____ 7. Based on this test, what is the necessary action?

_____

_____

# 84

# Fuel Pump Current Draw Test

**Meets NATEF Task:** (A8-D-3) Inspect and test fuel pump for pressure, regulation and volume; perform necessary action. (P-1)

---

**Name** Zach, Vamen     **Date** _____     **Time on Task** _____

**Make/Model** _____     **Year** _____     **Evaluation:** 4   3   2   1

✓ 1. Many electric fuel pumps can be measured for current draw in amperes. A higher than normal amperage draw may indicate a clogged fuel filter causing back pressure for the pump or a worn pump.

> **NOTE:** Other makes and models of vehicles can be tested by connecting the ammeter in series with the fuel pump fuse and then operating the engine. Check the wiring diagram for your specific vehicle.

✓ 2. Connect the digital multimeter, set to read amperes (A) and connect the red lead to the positive (+) of the battery. Connect the black lead to the fuel pump test terminal. The pump should run and an amperage reading should be observed on the meter. (Allow the pump to run for 30 seconds.) Confirm the reading with acceptable specifications.
Reading = ___7___ amp

Normal readings:     TBI = 2 to 5 amps (usually 9-13 psi)
                    Port injection = 4 to 8 amps (usually 35-45 psi)
                    Central port injection = 8 to 12 amps (55-64 psi)

- If the current is *lower* than specifications, check for:

     1. poor electrical connection at the fuel pump relay.
     2. poor connection at the fuel pump electrical connector.
     3. poor ground connection.
     4. defective fuel pressure regulator

- If the current is *higher* than specifications, check for:

     1. clogged fuel filter.
     2. pinched fuel lines.
     3. slowly rotating fuel pump.

✓ 3. Based on the test results, what is the necessary action?
nothing _____

# 85

# Fuel Pump Volume

**Meets NATEF Task:** (A8-D-3) Inspect and test fuel pump for pressure, regulation and volume; perform necessary action. (P-1)

Name **Zach, Warren**          Date _____          Time on Task _____

Make/Model _____          Year _____          Evaluation:  4  3  2  1

✓ **1.** Check service information for the recommended procedure to follow to determine fuel pump volume.

_____

_____

**How Fuel Pressure Affects Fuel Delivery At the Same Pulse Width**

**Fuel Volume Test**

✓ **2.** What is the specified volume? _____ (usually between 0.5 and 0.8 gallons per minute)

✓ **3.** What procedure was performed to determine fuel pump volume?

_____

**Fuel Loop**

✓ **4.** What was the fuel pump volume?

_____

✓ **5.** Based on the test results, what is the necessary action?

_____

_____

_____

# 86

# Fuel Pump Current Ramping

**Meets NATEF Task:** (A8-D-3) Inspect and test fuel pump for pressure, regulation and volume; perform necessary action. (P-1)

**Name** Zach, Warren     **Date** _____     **Time on Task** _____

**Make/Model** _____     **Year** _____     **Evaluation:** 4  3  2  1

_____ 1. Check service information for the specified fuel pump operating speed (normally from 3500 to 7500 RPM).

      _____

_____ 2. Tools and equipment needed to determine the rotational speed of the fuel pump include:

     _____ Digital storage oscilloscope

     _____ Current clamp

     _____ Fused jumper lead

_____ 3. Perform a current ramping procedure and determine the following:

     _____ Number of commentator segments = _____ (usually 8, 10, or 12)

     _____ Milliseconds needed for one rotation of the pump = _____

     _____ Fuel pump speed = 60,000 ÷ milliseconds = _____

_____ 4. Based on the test performed, what is the necessary action? _____

_____

# 87

# Clamp-On Meter Fuel Pump Current Draw

**Meets NATEF Task:** (A8-D-3) Inspect and test fuel pump for pressure, regulation and volume; perform necessary action. (P-1)

**Name** Zach, Warren **Date** _____ **Time on Task** _____

**Make/Model** _____ **Year** _____ **Evaluation: 4 3 2 1**

_____ **1.** Locate the fuel pump relay.

Location (describe) _____

_____ **2.** Remove the relay and determine the locations of the power (+) and load side (to the pump) terminals from the wiring diagram or label on the relay.

Battery voltage is at terminal (describe) 30 _____
(usually terminal #30)

Electric fuel pump is at terminal (describe) 87 _____
(usually terminal #87)

_____ **3.** Use a fused jumper wire with terminals that are properly sized for the relay socket and connect terminal #30 and #87.

_____ **4.** Set the digital multimeter to read DC amperes.

_____ **5.** Clamp the meter around the fused jumper wire and read the meter display.

_____7_____ amps

_____ **5.** Compare to the factory specifications. Specification = _____7_____ amp.

Most TBI (low pressure) fuel pumps (9-13 psi) ............2-5 amps
Most port fuel injection pumps (35-45 psi)...............4-8 amps
GM central port injection (trucks) (55-64 psi)...............8-12 amps

_____ **6.** Based on the test results, what is the necessary action? nothing _____

_____

# 88

# Fuel Filter Replacement

**Meets NATEF Task:** (A8-D-4) Replace fuel filter. (P-1)

**Name** _____ **Date** _____ **Time on Task** _____

**Make/Model** _____ **Year** _____ **Evaluation: 4  3  2  1**

_____ **1.** Check service information for the recommended part number and fuel filter replacement procedure.

      a. Fuel filter part number = _____

      b. Recommended procedure: _____

      _____

_____ **2.** Check all that apply:

    _____ Fuel system pressure should be relieved before removing the old filter

    _____ Special tools required to remove filter (describe): _____

    _____

    _____ Direction of fuel flow labeled on the filter? _____

    _____ Other (describe) _____

    _____

# 89

# Modes of Fuel Injection Operation

**Meets NATEF Task:** (A8-A-3) Research applicable vehicle and service information, such as engine management system operation, service history, service precautions, and TSBs. (P-1)

Name _____ Date _____ Time on Task _____

Make/Model _____ Year _____ Evaluation: 4  3  2  1

_____ **1.** Check service information for the sensors that are used to control the fuel injection system at each of the six modes of operation.

_____

_____ **2.** Starting cranking mode:

      **Sensors Used**                          **Why**

_____           _____

_____           _____

_____ **3.** Acceleration enrichment mode:

      **Sensors Used**                          **Why**

_____           _____

_____           _____

_____ **4.** Deceleration enleanment mode:

      **Sensors Used**                          **Why**

_____           _____

_____           _____

_____ **5.** Open-loop operation mode:

      **Sensors Used**                          **Why**

_____           _____

_____           _____

_____ **6.** Closed-loop operation mode:

      **Sensors Used**                          **Why**

_____           _____

_____           _____

_____ **7.** Fuel shut-off mode:

      **Sensors Used**                          **Why**

_____           _____

_____           _____

# 90

# Idle Air Control DMM Testing

**Meets NATEF Task:** (A8-B-5) Inspect and test sensors, actuators, and circuits using a graphing multimeter (GMM)/digital storage oscilloscope (DSO); perform necessary action. (P-1)

Name _____ Date _____ Time on Task _____

Make/Model _____ Year _____ Evaluation: 4 3 2 1

_____ 1. Check service information for the specified voltage and/or resistance specifications and testing procedures.

Voltage/resistance specifications: _____

_____

Specified testing procedures: _____

_____

_____ 2. List the steps performed and the test results obtained.

_____

_____

_____

_____

_____ 3. Do the sensor test results match the specifications?

_____ Yes _____ No (explain why not) _____

_____

_____

_____ 4. Based on the test results, what is the necessary action? _____

_____

_____

# 91

# Idle Air Control

**Meets NATEF Task:** (A8-B-7) Diagnose driveability and emissions problems resulting from malfunctions of interrelated systems, etc.; perform necessary action. (P-3)

---

Name _____ Date _____ Time on Task _____

Make/Model _____ Year _____ Evaluation: 4 3 2 1

The idle air control is used to control idle speed by increasing or decreasing the amount of air entering the engine similar to what occurs when the accelerator pedal is depressed.

_____ **1.** Connect a scan tool.

_____ **2.** Look at the IAC commanded position = _____ (should be 15 to 25% or counts on a warm engine in park or neutral).

       **OK** ____ **NOT OK** ____

**Diagnosis:**

- **IAC counts higher than normal.** This could indicate one or more of the following:
    1. Engine not fully warm
    2. Some electrical load is on, such as daytime running lights or air conditioning
    3. Dirty throttle plates
    4. Abnormal load on the engine
- **IAC counts lower than normal.** This could indicate one or more of the following:
    1. A vacuum leak
    2. Misadjusted idle speed control
    3. Stuck or binding throttle cable or linkage

_____ **3.** Based on the inspection of the system, what is the necessary action? _____

# 92

# Inspect Air Induction System for Leaks

**Meets NATEF Task:** (A8-D-5) Inspect throttle body, air induction system, intake manifold and gaskets for vacuum leaks and/or unmetered air. (P-2)

---

**Name** _____  **Date** _____  **Time on Task** _____

**Make/Model** _____  **Year** _____  **Evaluation:** 4  3  2  1

_____ **1.** Check service information for the recommended procedure to locate vacuum leaks and/or unmetered air.

_____

_____

CHECK THE
SNORKEL TUBE
HERE FOR
CRACKS.

_____ **2.** The recommended procedure includes the following. Check all that apply.

     _____ Checking IAC counts

     _____ Using throttle body cleaner or propane

     _____ Using smoke

     _____ Other (describe) _____

     _____

Low Engine Vacuum

False/Unmetered Air

Throttle Plate

False/Unmetered Air

_____ **3.** Based on the tests and inspection, were air induction leaks found and, if so, describe the location.

_____

_____

# 93

We Support
NATEF

# Air Intake Inspection

**Meets NATEF Task:** (A8-D-5) Inspect throttle body, air induction system, intake manifold and gaskets for vacuum leaks and/or unmetered air. (P-2)

Name _____ Date _____ Time on Task _____

Make/Model _____ Year _____ Evaluation: 4  3  2  1

Every engine takes in a large quantity of air during its operation. If the air stream leading to the engine is restricted or otherwise defective, the engine will not perform correctly.

_____ **1.** Locate and remove the air filter.

        a.  Did it fit snugly in the housing? **YES ___ NO ___**

        b.  Is the filter wet or deformed? **YES ___ NO ___**

_____ **2.** Inspect the filter for restriction or breaks.

        **OK _____ NOT OK _____**

_____ **3.** Is a new air filter required? **YES ___ NO ___**

_____ **4.** Inspect the air duct work from the filter to the outside air source.

        a.  Is the passageway open and clean? **YES ___ NO ___**

        b.  Is the duct work okay and free from tears or holes? **YES ___ NO ___**

_____ **5.** Inspect the air duct work from the filter to the engine inlet.

        a.  Is the duct work okay and free from tears or holes? **YES ___ NO ___**

# 94

# Gasoline Direct Injection Identification

**Meets NATEF Task:** (A8-A-3) Research applicable vehicle and service information, such as engine management system operation, vehicle service history, and TSBs. (P-1)

Name _____ Date _____ Time on Task _____

Make/Model _____ Year _____ Evaluation: 4 3 2 1

_____ **1.** Check service information to determine if the vehicle being serviced is equipped with gasoline direct injection. (check all that apply)

       ____ Gasoline direct injection only

       ____ Port and gasoline direct injection system

_____ **2.** List the specifications as found in service information.

       a. Lift pump pressure = _____

       b. Lift pump volume = _____

       c. High-pressure system pressure = _____

       d. Fuel injector resistance = _____

       e. Other (describe) _____

_____ **3.** What is the specified maintenance procedures required (if any)? Describe:

_____

_____

# 95

# Electronic Throttle Control System ID

**Meets NATEF Task:** (A8-A-3) Research applicable vehicle and service information, such as engine management system operation, vehicle service history, and TSBs. (P-1)

Name _____    Date _____    Time on Task _____

Make/Model _____    Year _____    Evaluation:  4  3  2  1

_____ 1. Check service information to determine if the vehicle being serviced is equipped with an electronic throttle control (ETC) system. Describe how it was determined. (check all that apply)

         _____ Visual inspection

         _____ Service information

         _____ Scan tool

         _____ Other (describe) _____

_____ 2. Does the electronic throttle control system use a cable between the accelerator pedal and the APP sensor?

         _____ Yes        _____ No

_____ 3. What is the relearn procedure that needs to be followed if the electronic throttle control system throttle body assembly is replaced? Describe the specified procedure.

         _____

         _____

# 96

# Idle Air Control DMM Testing

**Meets NATEF Task:** (A8-B-5) Inspect and test computerized engine control system sensors, PCM/ECM, actuators, and circuits using a GMM/DSO; perform necessary action. (P-1)

---

Name _____ Date _____ Time on Task _____

Make/Model _____ Year _____ Evaluation: 4 3 2 1

_____ 1. Check service information for the specified voltage and/or resistance specifications and testing procedures.

Voltage/resistance specifications: _____

_____

Specified testing procedures: _____

_____

_____ 2. List the steps performed and the test results obtained.

_____

_____

_____

_____

_____ 3. Do the sensor test results match the specifications?

_____ Yes _____ No (explain why not) _____

_____

_____

_____ 4. Based on the test results, what is the necessary action? _____

_____

_____

# 97

# Position Sensor Visual Inspection

**Meets NATEF Task:** (A8-B-6) Access and use service information to perform step-by-step diagnosis. (P-1)

---

**Name** _____ **Date** _____ **Time on Task** _____

**Make/Model** _____ **Year** _____ **Evaluation: 4 3 2 1**

_____ 1. Check service information for the location, wire colors, and specified testing procedures for the position sensor.

     Location: _____

     Wire colors and purpose: _____

     _____

     Recommended testing procedure: _____

     _____

_____ 2. Describe the actual location of the position sensor. _____

_____ 3. Verify the wire colors and the location in the electrical connector.

     **OK** ____ **NOT OK** ____ Describe fault: _____

     _____

_____ 4. Check the condition of the electrical terminals.

     **OK** ____ **NOT OK** ____ Describe fault: _____

     _____

_____ 5. Check the physical condition of the sensor for signs of contamination or damage.

     **OK** ____ **NOT OK** ____ Describe fault: _____

     _____

_____ 6. Based on the inspection, what is the necessary action? _____

     _____

# 98

# Position Sensor Diagnosis

**Meets NATEF Task:** (A8-B-6) Access and use service information to perform step-by-step diagnosis. (P-1)

Name _____ Date _____ Time on Task _____

Make/Model _____ Year _____ Evaluation:  4  3  2  1

_____ 1. Check service information for the type of sensor used for the crankshaft position (CKP) and the camshaft position (CMP).

      CKP – Describe the type of sensor _____

      CMP – Describe the type of sensor _____

_____ 2. Check service information and determine the recommended testing procedures for testing the CKP sensor.

      Wire colors and their purpose:

      Wire #1 _____

      Wire #2 _____

      Wire #3 _____

      Recommended testing procedure and specifications: _____

      _____

      Test results: _____ OK _____ NOT OK _____

_____ 3. Check service information and determine the recommended testing procedures for testing the CMP sensor.

      Wire colors and their purpose:

      Wire #1 _____

      Wire #2 _____

      Wire #3 _____

      Recommended testing procedure and specifications: _____

      _____

      Test results: _____ OK _____ NOT OK _____

_____ 4. Based on the test results, what is the necessary action? _____

# 99

# Position Sensor Waveform Testing

**Meets NATEF Task:** (A8-B-6) Access and use service information to perform step-by-step diagnosis. (P-1)

Name _____ Date _____ Time on Task _____

Make/Model _____ Year _____ Evaluation: 4 3 2 1

_____ **1.** Check service information regarding the location and type of position sensors used on the vehicle being tested.

                           **Crankshaft Position (CKP) Camshaft Position (CMP)**

Location (describe):          _____ _____

Type of sensor (Hall-Effect,
magnetic, etc.):               _____ _____

CKP signal
0.5 VAC Minimum
CMP signal
5.0 VDC
60° BTDC Cylinder #1   TDC Cylinder #1 Compression Stroke      60° BTDC Cylinder #1

_____ **2.** Check service information for the wire colors used and their purpose.

                           **Crankshaft Position (CKP)**    **Camshaft Position (CMP)**

Wire 1 (color and purpose): _____ _____

Wire 2 (color and purpose): _____ _____

Wire 3 (color and purpose): _____ _____

_____ **3.** Check service information for the specified voltage output and/or waveform for the CKP and CMP sensors.

     CKP _____         CMP _____

_____ **4.** Following the test equipment manufacturer's instructions, show the instructor the waveforms.    CKP – Instructor OK _____    CMP – Instructor OK _____

_____ **5.** Based on the comparison between the captured waveform and the specified waveform, what action is needed?

_____

# 100

# Crankshaft/Camshaft Sensor Scan Tool Diagnosis

**Meets NATEF Task:** (A8-B-6) Access and use service information to perform step-by-step diagnosis. (P-1)

Name _____ Date _____ Time on Task _____

Make/Model _____ Year _____ Evaluation: 4 3 2 1

_____ 1. Check service information for the specified method of checking and relearning the crankshaft position (CKP) and the camshaft position (CMP) sensors.

_____

_____

_____ 2. According to service information, when should the crankshaft/camshaft position be relearned?

_____

_____

_____ 3. Use a scan tool and follow the instructions for the crankshaft and/or camshaft learn procedure.

_____

_____

_____

_____

```
Engine Data 1
CMP Retard                    -6 °
Engine Speed                626 RP
Desired Idle Speed          625 RP
IAC Position                 59 Co
Desired IAC Position         58 Co
ECT Sensor                  154 °F
IAT Sensor                   64 °
MAF Sensor                 5.52 g
Desired IAC Airflow        5.69 g
```

_____ 4. What are the specifications for the crankshaft/camshaft position sensors?

_____

_____ 5. Based on the test results, what is the necessary action? _____

_____

# 101

# Scan Tool Diagnosis

**Meets NATEF Task:** (A8-B-7) Diagnose driveability and emissions problems resulting from malfunctions of interrelated systems; determine necessary action. (P-3)

Name _____ Date _____ Time on Task _____

Make/Model _____ Year _____ Evaluation: 4 3 2 1

(Not all of this data will be available on all vehicles or scan tools - if not available, put N.A.)

_____ 1. DTCs: _____ Pending DTC:_____

_____ 2. Engine coolant temperature (ECT): cold _____ warm _____

_____ 3. Intake air temperature (IAT): cold _____ warm _____

_____ 4. Upstream O2S1: lowest voltage observed _____ highest voltage observed _____

_____ 5. Upstream O2S2: lowest voltage observed _____ highest voltage observed _____

_____ 6. Downstream O2S: lowest voltage observed _____ highest voltage observed _____

_____ 7. $O_2$ cross counts: @ idle____ @ 2,000 RPM____

_____ 8. Injector pulse width: @ idle (park)_____ @ idle (drive)_____

@ 2,000 RPM (park)_____ @ 3,000 RPM (park)_____

_____ 9. Spark advance: @ idle (park)_____ @ idle (drive)_____

@ 2,000 RPM (park)_____ @ 3,000 RPM (park)_____

_____10. Short term fuel trim (integrator): @ idle (park)_____

@ idle (drive)_____ @ 2,000 RPM (park)_____

_____11. Long term fuel trim (block learn): @ idle (park)_____ @ idle (drive)_____

_____12. P/S switch: OK_____ NOT OK_____

_____13. MAP: @ idle (park)_____ @ idle (drive)_____

_____14. MAF (grams/sec): @ idle (park)_____ @ idle (drive)_____

@ 2,000 RPM (park)_____ @ key on (engine off)_____

_____15. IAC counts: @ idle (park)_____ @ idle (drive)_____

@ A/C on (drive)_____ @ 2,000 RPM (park)_____

_____16. Throttle position (TP) sensor: @ idle____ @ W.O.T. engine off, ignition "on"_____

_____17. Battery voltage:_____

_____18. Troubles with the vehicle? (if any)_____

# 102

# Fuel Trim Diagnosis

**Meets NATEF Task:** (A8-B-7) Diagnose driveability and emissions problems resulting from malfunctions of interrelated systems; determine necessary action. (P-3)

---

**Name** _____ **Date** _____ **Time on Task** _____

**Make/Model** _____ **Year** _____ **Evaluation:** 4  3  2  1

Fuel trim is the computer correction factor that uses the oxygen sensor to determine if more or less fuel needs to be delivered by the fuel injectors. Fuel trim is only available on a scan tool.

_____ 1. Connect a scan tool and select long-term fuel trim (LTFT) (block learn) and short-term fuel trim (STFT).

_____ 2. Start the engine and operate until normal operating temperature and closed loop status is achieved.

_____ 3. Record the following cell number and LTFT amount:

| | Cell | LTFT | STFT |
|---|---|---|---|
| Idle in Drive (if automatic transmission only) | _____ | _____ | _____ |
| Idle in Park A/C off | _____ | _____ | _____ |
| Idle in Park A/C on | _____ | _____ | _____ |
| 3000 RPM in Park | _____ | _____ | _____ |

Results: Fuel trim should be within plus or minus 10% or within 118-138 if the block/integration is displayed as a binary number.

_____ 4. Based on the test results, what is the necessary action? _____

_____

103

# IAC Scan Tool Diagnosis

**Meets NATEF Task:** (A8-B-8) Perform active tests of actuators using a scan tool; determine necessary action. (P-1)

Name _____ Date _____ Time on Task _____

Make/Model _____ Year _____ Evaluation: 4 3 2 1

_____ **1.** Check service information for the specified IAC position as displayed on a scan tool.

_____

_____

_____ **2.** Check service information for the units used to express the position of the IAC.

_____ Counts

_____ Percentage (%)

_____ Milliamperes (mA)

_____ Other (describe) _____

```
                Engine Data 1
CMP Retard                        -6 °
Engine Speed                     626 RP
Desired Idle Speed               625 RP
IAC Position                      59 Co
Desired IAC Position              58 Co
ECT Sensor                       154 °
IAT Sensor                        64 °
MAF Sensor                       5.52 g
Desired IAC Airflow              5.69 g
                                  1 /
```

_____ **3.** What is the IAC position on a fully warmed engine without any accessories on?

_____

_____ **4.** Create a vacuum leak. How does the IAC react?

_____ IAC position decreased (usually for speed density-equipped engines)

_____ IAC position increases (usually for engines equipped with a MAF sensor)

_____ **5.** Based on the test results, what is the necessary action? _____

_____

# 104

# Port Fuel-Injection System Diagnosis

**Meets NATEF Task:** (A8-D-1) Diagnose hot or cold no-starting, hard starting, poor driveability, and etc.; determine necessary action (P-1)

Name _____ Date _____ Time on Task _____

Make/Model _____ Year _____ Evaluation: 4 3 2 1

_____ 1. Check service information for the recommended procedure to follow to diagnose the fuel injection system.

_____ 2. Attach a fuel pressure gauge to the Schrader valve on the fuel rail, if available.

_____ 3. Turn the ignition key to "on" or start the engine to build up the fuel pump pressure.

_____ psi (should reach specified fuel pressure, usually about 35-45 psi)

_____ 4. Turn the ignition off and wait 20 minutes and observe the fuel pressure retained in the fuel rail = _____ psi. If the drop is less than 20 psi in 20 minutes, everything is OK. (The fuel pressure should *not* drop more than 20 psi in 20 minutes.)

If the drop is *greater* than 20 psi in 20 minutes, there is a possible problem with:

    a. the check valve in the fuel pump.
    b. leaking injectors.
    c. a defective (leaking) fuel pressure regulator.

To determine which unit is defective, perform the following:

| | |
|---|---|
| Step #1: | Re-energize the electric fuel pump. |
| Step #2: | Clamp the fuel *supply* line, wait 10 minutes. If the pressure drop does *not* occur - replace the fuel pump. If the pressure drop still occurs - continue with Step #3. |
| Step #3: | Repeat the pressure build up of the electric pump and clamp the fuel return line. If the pressure drop time is now OK, replace the fuel pressure regulator. |
| Step #4: | If the pressure drop still occurs, the injectors are leaking. Remove the injectors with the fuel rail and hold over paper. Replace those injectors that drip a drop or more after 10 minutes with pressurized fuel. |

**CAUTION:** Do not clamp plastic fuel lines. Connect shut-off valves to the fuel system to shut off supply and return lines.

_____ 5. Based on the test results, what is the necessary action? _____

# 105

# Fuel Injection Stethoscope Test

**Meets NATEF Task:** (A8-D-1) Diagnose problems associated with engine operation or vehicles equipped with injection-type fuel systems; determine necessary action (P-1)

Name _____ Date _____ Time on Task _____

Make/Model _____ Year _____ Evaluation: 4 3 2 1

_____ **1.** Using a stethoscope, listen to the sound of each injector with the engine running at idle speed. They should all make the same clicking sound.

_____ All injectors make the same sound

_____ One injector makes a different sound from the others

_____ More than one injector makes a different sound than the others

_____ **2.** Listen for fuel flow returning to the fuel tank from the fuel pressure regulator.

_____ **OK** – can hear fuel returning to the tank

_____ **NOT OK** – may be a fuel pressure regulator fault or a weak fuel pump

_____ **3.** Based on the test results, what is the necessary action? _____

_____

# 106

# Injector Balance Testing

**Meets NATEF Task:** (A8-D-1) Diagnose problems associated with engine operation or vehicles equipped with injection-type fuel systems; determine necessary action (P-1)

---

Name _____ Date _____ Time on Task _____

Make/Model _____ Year _____ Evaluation: 4  3  2  1

### (Ohmmeter Method)

_____ **1.** Check service information for the specified injector resistance. _____


_____ **2.** Measure the resistance of all injectors with a digital ohmmeter.

> **NOTE:** For best performance and idle quality, all injectors should measure within 0.3 to 0.4 ohms of each other.

Injector resistance:

| Resistance | Resistance |
|------------|------------|
| 1. _____ | 5. _____ |
| 2. _____ | 6. _____ |
| 3. _____ | 7. _____ |
| 4. _____ | 8. _____ |

Digital Ohmmeter

Connect Leads Across Injector Terminals

Highest resistance = _____ ohms.

Lowest resistance = _____ ohms.

Difference        = _____ ohms (should be less than 0.4 ohms).

OK_____    NOT OK_____

# 107

# Fuel Injection System Diagnosis

**Meets NATEF Task:** (A8-D-1) Diagnose problems associated with engine operation or vehicles equipped with injection-type fuel systems; determine necessary action (P-1)

Name _Zach, Warren_    Date _____    Time on Task _____

Make/Model _____    Year _____    Evaluation: 4 3 2 1

✓ **1.** Check service information for the recommended diagnosis procedure to follow when diagnosing fuel injection faults.

_____

_____

✓ **2.** List the components included in the fuel injection system.

    a. _fuel pump_

    b. _fuel pump relay_

    c. _fuel rail_

    d. _fuel filter_

    e. _fuel injectors_

    f. _fuel pressure regulator_

    g. _fuel tank_

    h. _fuel lines_

    j. _fuel neck_

✓ **3.** What measurements are specified? Check all that apply.

    a. Fuel pressure

    b. Injector resistance

    c. Injector pressure drop

    d. Other (describe) _____

✓ **4.** Based on the symptoms and the recommended diagnostic procedures, what is the necessary action?

_nothing_

_____

# 108

# Inspect Air Induction System for Leaks

**Meets NATEF Task:** (A8-D-5) Inspect throttle body, air induction system, intake manifold and gaskets for vacuum leaks and/or unmetered air. (P-2)

Name _____ Date _____ Time on Task _____

Make/Model _____ Year _____ Evaluation: 4 3 2 1

_____ **1.** Check service information for the recommended procedure to locate vacuum leaks and/or unmetered air.

_____

_____

CHECK THE SNORKEL TUBE HERE FOR CRACKS.

_____ **2.** The recommended procedure includes the following. Check all that apply.

_____ Checking IAC counts

_____ Using throttle body cleaner or propane

_____ Using smoke

_____ Other (describe) _____

_____

Low Engine Vacuum

False/Unmetered Air

Throttle Plate

False/Unmetered Air

_____ **3.** Based on the tests and inspection, were air induction leaks found and, if so, describe the location.

_____

_____

# 109

We Support
NATEF

# Injector Pressure Drop Testing

**Meets NATEF Task:** (A8-D-6) Inspect and test fuel injectors. (P-1)

Name _____ Date _____ Time on Task _____

Make/Model _____ Year _____ Evaluation: 4 3 2 1

_____ 1. Check service information for the procedures and specifications for an injector pressure drop test.

_____

_____

     a. Part number of recommended tester = _____

     b. Maximum allowable variation in pressure drop among the injectors = _____

_____ 2. What was the starting fuel pressure?

     _____ psi/kPa

_____ 3. Record the pressure drop of the injectors.

     Cylinder #1 _____    Cylinder #5 _____

     Cylinder #2 _____    Cylinder #6 _____

     Cylinder #3 _____    Cylinder #7 _____

     Cylinder #4 _____    Cylinder #8 _____

_____ 4. Compare the test results with the specifications. What is the necessary action?

_____

_____

# 110

# Fuel Injector Balance Test

**Meets NATEF Task:** (A8-D-6) Inspect and test fuel injectors. (P-1)

Name _____ Date _____ Time on Task _____

Make/Model _____ Year _____ Evaluation: 4 3 2 1

**(Voltage Drop Method)**

_____ 1. Check service information for the procedures and specifications for an injector voltage drop test.

_____

_____

    a. Part number of recommended tester = _____

    b. Maximum allowable variation in voltage drop among the injectors = _____

_____ 2. What was the starting pressure?

    _____ psi/kPa

_____ 3. Record the voltage drop of the injectors (pressure after injector was pulsed on).

    Cylinder #1 _____     Cylinder #5 _____

    Cylinder #2 _____     Cylinder #6 _____

    Cylinder #3 _____     Cylinder #7 _____

    Cylinder #4 _____     Cylinder #8 _____

_____ 4. Compare the test results with the specifications. What is the necessary action?

_____

_____

# Injector Available Voltage

**Meets NATEF Task:** (A8-D-6) Inspect and test fuel injectors. (P-1)

Name _Zach, Warren_   Date _____   Time on Task _____

Make/Model _____   Year _____   Evaluation: 4 3 2 1

✓ 1. Check service information for the specified voltage at the fuel injectors.

   Specified voltage = _____

to Voltage     to PCM

Injector Electrical Connections

A B

✓ 2. Check service information for the maximum allowable voltage drop of the power side of the fuel injector circuit.

   Maximum voltage drop = _____

✓ 3. Perform a voltage drop test between the positive terminal of the battery and the fuel injector(s).

   Measured voltage drop for the injector on:

   Cylinder #1 _____        Cylinder #5 _____
   Cylinder #2 _____        Cylinder #6 _____
   Cylinder #3 _____        Cylinder #7 _____
   Cylinder #4 _____        Cylinder #8 _____

✓ 4. Based on the test results, what is the necessary action? _____

   _____

   _____

# 112

# Injector Voltage Waveform Test

**Meets NATEF Task:** (A8-D-6) Inspect and test fuel injectors. (P-1)

**Name** _Zach Warren_ **Date** _____ **Time on Task** _____

**Make/Model** _____ **Year** _____ **Evaluation:** 4 3 2 1

____ **1.** Check service information for the type of fuel injector being used.

　　　　____ Saturated

　　　　____ Peak and hold

____ **2.** Connect a digital storage oscilloscope (DSO) or graphing multimeter (GMM) to the pulsed side of the injector. (Check service information for the color of wire used for the pulse.)

____ **3.** Start the engine and observe the voltage waveform.

**Injector Voltage**

15.0 V

0.0 V

**Voltage in Injector Circuit**

Peak　　Hold

Fuel Injector

____ **4.** Does the voltage spike (kick) exceed 30 volts? ____ Yes ____ No

____ **5.** What is the injector pulse-width? _____ (normally between 1.5 and 3.5 mS at idle on a warm engine)

____ **6.** Based on the test performed, what is the necessary action? _Nothing_

_____

_____

# 113

# Injector Current Ramping

**Meets NATEF Task:** (A8-D-6) Inspect and test fuel injectors. (P-1)

Name _Zach, Warren_     Date _____     Time on Task _____

Make/Model _____     Year _____     Evaluation: 4 3 2 1

✓    **1.** Check service information for the type of fuel injector being used.

       _____ Saturated

       _____ Peak and hold

✓    **2.** Connect a digital storage oscilloscope (DSO) or graphing multimeter (GMM) to the pulsed side of the injector. (Check service information for the color of wire used for the pulse.)

✓    **3.** Start the engine and observe the current waveform.

✓    **4.** Does the current waveform correct?    ✓ _____ Yes    _____ No

✓    **5.** What is the injector pulse-width? _____ (normally between 1.5 and 3.5 ms at idle on a warm engine)

✓    **6.** Based on the test performed, what is the necessary action? _____

_____

# Single Line Fuel Injector Cleaning

**Meets NATEF Task:** (A8-D-6) Inspect and test fuel injectors. (P-1)

---

**Name** _____ **Date** _____ **Time on Task** _____

**Make/Model** _____ **Year** _____ **Evaluation:** 4 3 2 1

_____ **1.** Check service information for the recommended injector cleaning method.

_____

_____

_____

_____ **2.** Equipment or supplies needed to clean fuel injectors as specified by the vehicle manufacturer include:

   a. _____

   b. _____

   c. _____

   d. _____

   e. _____

   f. _____

_____ **3.** Following the instructions on the fuel injector cleaning equipment, perform the injector cleaning.

_____ **4.** Describe what difference in engine operation was noticed after the fuel injectors were cleaned.

_____

_____

# 115

# Dual Line Fuel Injector Cleaning

**Meets NATEF Task:** (A8-D-6) Inspect and test fuel injectors. (P-1)

Name _____ Date _____ Time on Task _____

Make/Model _____ Year _____ Evaluation: 4 3 2 1

_____ 1. Check service information for the recommended injector cleaning method.

_____

_____

_____

_____ 2. Equipment or supplies needed to clean fuel injectors as specified by the vehicle
manufacturer include:

a. _____

b. _____

c. _____

d. _____

e. _____

f. _____

Cleaning Injector Rail

Fuel Loop
Disconnected
from Rail and
Looped Back

_____ 3. Following the instructions on the fuel injector cleaning equipment, perform the
injector cleaning.

_____ 4. Describe what difference in engine operation was noticed after the fuel injectors were
cleaned.

_____

_____

# 116

# Minimum Air Adjustment

**Meets NATEF Task:** (A8-D-7)  Verify idle control operation.  (P-1)

Name _____  Date _____  Time on Task _____

Make/Model _____  Year _____  Evaluation:  4  3  2  1

_____ 1. Check service information for the specified procedure to follow to check and adjust minimum air (minimum idle speed) adjustment.

_____

_____

_____ 2. Specifications usually include the following steps (check all that apply):

_____ Engine at normal operating temperature

_____ Seat IAC

_____ Disconnect the electrical connector and IAC

_____ Connect the scan tool or tachometer to monitor engine speed (RPM)

_____ Compare reading to specifications

_____ Other (describe) _____

_____

_____ 3. Specifications for minimum air (idle) = _____

_____ 4. Minimum air (idle) results before adjustment = _____

_____ 5. What action is needed?

_____

_____

_____

Idle Speed

# 117

# Vehicle Emission Rating

**Meets NATEF Task**: (A8-A-3)  Research applicable vehicle and service information.
(P-1)

Name _____  Date _____  Time on Task _____

Make/Model _____  Year _____  Evaluation:  4  3  2  1

_____  **1.** Check service information and/or the vehicle emission control information (VECI) label under the hood to determine national and California standards. (check all that apply)

### National Standard

_____ Tier 1

_____ Tier 2

_____ Bin (list number) _____

### California Standard

_____ TLEV

_____ LEV (LEV I)

_____ ULEV

_____ SULEV

_____ ZEV

_____ PZEV

_____ ILEV

_____ AT-PZEV

_____ NLEV

_____  **2.** Define the specified rating. _____

_____

_____

# 118

# Exhaust Gas Analysis

**Meets NATEF Task:** (A8-A-13) Prepare 4 or 5 gas analyzer; inspect and prepare vehicle for test, and obtain exhaust readings; interpret readings, and determine necessary action  (P-3)

Name _____   Date _____   Time on Task _____

Make/Model _____   Year _____   Evaluation:  4  3  2  1

_____ **1.** Check the instruction information for the exhaust gas analyzer being used to determine the proper test procedures to follow.

_____

_____

_____ **2.** Check the vehicle for exhaust leaks and other faults that could affect the exhaust gas readings.

_____

_____ **3.** Prepare the vehicle for testing, which usually includes operating the engine until normal operating temperature has been achieved. List other items listed by the test equipment manufacturer that should be performed.

_____

_____

_____ **4.** Obtain the exhaust gas readings and compare them to specifications.

| Gas | Idle | 2500 RPM | General Specifications |
|---|---|---|---|
| HC | | | Max 50 PPM |
| CO | | | Max 0.5% |
| $CO_2$ | | | 12% to 15% or higher |
| $O_2$ | | | 0% to 2% |
| $NO_X$ | | | Less than 100 PPM @ idle Less than 1000 PPM @ wide open throttle |

_____ **5.** Based on the exhaust gas readings, what is the necessary action?

_____

# 119

# Diagnosis of Emission-Related Concerns

**Meets NATEF Task:** (A8-B-3) Diagnose the causes of emissions or driveability concerns resulting from malfunctions in the computerized engine control system with stored diagnostic trouble codes. (P-1)

Name _____    Date _____    Time on Task _____

Make/Model _____    Year _____    Evaluation: 4  3  2  1

_____ 1. Check service information for the specified methods to follow to determine the cause of an emission-related concern with stored diagnostic trouble codes.

_____

_____

_____

_____

_____

_____

_____ 2. Following the vehicle manufacturer's recommended procedure, retrieve the stored DTC(s).

| DTC | Description of DTC | Possible Causes |
|-----|--------------------|-----------------|
|     |                    |                 |
|     |                    |                 |
|     |                    |                 |

_____ 3. What emission concerns could result from faults indicated by the DTCs?

_____

_____

_____ 4. Based on the test results and service information, what is the necessary action?

_____

# 120

We Support
ASE NATEF

# EVAP System Component Inspection

**Meet NATEF Task:** (A8-E-10) Diagnose emissions and driveability concerns caused by the evaporative emissions control system; determine necessary action. (P-1)

Name _____ Date _____ Time on Task _____

Make/Model _____ Year _____ Evaluation: 4 3 2 1

_____ 1. According to the underhood emission label, with what type of system is the vehicle equipped?

        _____ Pre-OBD I (1987 or older)

        _____ OBD I (1988-1995)

        _____ OBD II (1996 and newer)

        _____ Unknown (describe) _____

_____ 2. Check the service information and the vehicle emission label for the following information.

       a. The location of the carbon canister

         (describe) _____

         _____

       b. The location of the purge control

         solenoid(s) (describe) _____

         _____

       c. The resistance specification for the evaporator control solenoid(s) = _____

_____ 3. Visually inspect the following items and check for any sign of a leak in the system.

       a. Canister hoses      **OK** _____      **NOT OK** _____

       b. Gas cap           **OK** _____      **NOT OK** _____

_____ 4. Based on the inspection, what is the necessary action?

       _____

# 121

# Evaporative Emission Controls Diagnosis

**Meets NATEF Task:** (A8-E-11) Inspect and test components and hoses of the evaporative emissions control system; perform necessary action. (P-1)

Name _____ Date _____ Time on Task _____

Make/Model _____ Year _____ Evaluation: 4 3 2 1

_____ 1. Check service information for the specified tests and procedures to follow to diagnose the problems in the evaporative emission control system.

_____

_____

_____

_____ 2. List the tools and equipment specified for use by service information. Check all that apply.

   _____ Special tester (describe) _____

   _____ Scan tool

   _____ Other (describe) _____

_____ 3. List the components included in the evaporative emission control unit and describe how each is to be tested according to service information.

|  | Component | Test or Inspection |
|---|---|---|
| a. | _____ | _____ |
| b. | _____ | _____ |
| c. | _____ | _____ |
| d. | _____ | _____ |

_____ 4. Based on the results of the tests and inspection, what is the necessary action?

_____

# EVAP System Scan Tool Testing

**Meets NATEF Task:** (A8-E-11)  Inspect and test components and hoses of the evaporative emissions control system; perform necessary action.  (P-1)

Name _____    Date _____    Time on Task _____

Make/Model _____    Year _____    Evaluation:  4   3   2   1

_____ **1.** Check service information for the recommended checks and test procedures to follow when diagnosing the EVAP system using a scan tool.

_____

_____

_____ **2.** List the solenoids that can be commanded on or off using a scan tool. (Note: The factory scan tool or an enhanced version of an aftermarket scan tool may be necessary to provide bi-directional control of the components in the EVAP system.)

| Component | Command ON/Off? |
|---|---|
| _____ | _____ |
| _____ | _____ |
| _____ | _____ |
| _____ | _____ |

_____ **3.** Using the scan tool, what EVAP-related data (PID) is displayed?

| PID | Value Displayed |
|---|---|
| _____ | _____ |
| _____ | _____ |
| _____ | _____ |
| _____ | _____ |

_____ **4.** Based on the test results using a scan tool, what is the necessary action? _____

_____

# 123

# Canister Purge Flow Rate Test

**Meets NATEF Task:** (A8-E-11) Inspect and test components and hoses of the evaporative emissions control system; perform necessary action. (P-1)

Name _____ Date _____ Time on Task _____

Make/Model _____ Year _____ Evaluation: 4  3  2  1

_____ **1.** Check service information for the purge flow rate specifications and test procedures.

_____

_____

Purge flow rate (usually a minimum of one liter per minute) = _____

When does purge occur? _____

_____ **2.** Convert the designated purge flow rate gauge to the charcoal canister following the instructions of the tester.

_____

Purge flow rate = _____ liters per minute

____ **OK**    ____ **NOT OK**

_____ **3.** Based on the purge flow test results,
what is the necessary action? _____

_____

_____

_____

_____

RUBBER
HOSE

LITER/MIN
10
9
8
7
6
5
4
3
2
1

CLEAR PLASTIC
FLOW GAUGE

LOCATION OF STEEL
BALL INDICATES
AMOUNT OF CANISTER
PURGE IN LITERS
PER MINUTE

TO MANIFOLD

RUBBER HOSE

CHARCOAL
CANISTER

# 124

# Smoke Test of the EVAP System

**Meets NATEF Task:** (A8-E-11) Inspect and test components and hoses of the evaporative emissions control system; perform necessary action. (P-1)

Name _____ Date _____ Time on Task _____

Make/Model _____ Year _____ Evaluation: 4 3 2 1

_____ 1. Check service information for the procedures and pressures to follow when checking the evaporative emission control system for leaks using smoke.

_____

_____

Specified maximum pressure = _____

_____ 2. Connect the smoke machine to the evaporative emission control system following the instructions supplied with the smoke machine.

_____

_____

_____

_____

_____ 3. Use a bright light and look for smoke leaking from the evaporative emission control system. Describe the leaks, if any.

_____

_____

_____ 4. Based on the results of the smoke testing, what is the necessary action? _____

_____

# 125

# Evaporative Emission DTC Diagnosis

**Meets NATEF Task:** (A8-E-12) Interpret diagnostic trouble codes (DTCs) and scan tool data related to the emissions control systems; determine necessary action. (P-1)

Name _____ Date _____ Time on Task _____

Make/Model _____ Year _____ Evaluation: 4  3  2  1

_____ **1.** Check service information for the specified diagnostic steps to follow if evaporative emission control-related DTC(s) is set.

_____

_____

_____ **2.** Describe the test and inspection specified for each of the DTCs listed.

| DTC | Specified Test(s) |
|-----|-------------------|
| P0440 | _____ |
| P0441 | _____ |
| P0442 | _____ |
| Other (list) | _____ |
| Other (list) | _____ |

_____ **3.** Based on the results of the tests and inspection, what is the necessary action?

_____

# 126

# EGR System Diagnosis

**Meets NATEF Task:** (A8-E-3) Diagnose emissions and driveability concerns caused by the exhaust gas recirculation (EGR) system; determine necessary action. (P-1)

___

Name _____ Date _____ Time on Task _____

Make/Model _____ Year _____ Evaluation: 4  3  2  1

_____ **1.** Check service information for the specified testing procedure of the exhaust gas recirculation (EGR) system using a scan tool.

_____

_____

_____ **2.** List the EGR-related data that can be retrieved using a scan tool.

_____

_____ **3.** List the scan tool commands (bi-directional) for the EGR system and describe the results of the tests.

| **Unit Commanded** | **Results** |
|---|---|
| _____ | _____ |
| _____ | _____ |
| _____ | _____ |

_____ **4.** Has the EGR OBD II monitor run? _____

_____ **5.** Based on the results of the scan tool diagnosis, what is the necessary action?

_____

_____

_____

_____

_____

# 127

# Service EGR System

**Meets NATEF Task:** (A8-E-4) Inspect, test, service and replace components of the EGR system, exhaust passages, vacuum/pressure controls, filters and hoses; perform necessary action. (P-1)

---

Name _____ Date _____ Time on Task _____

Make/Model _____ Year _____ Evaluation: 4  3  2  1

The EGR passages and valve that control the flow of exhaust gases can become clogged with carbon. The EGR valve and passages may need to be cleaned if one or more of the following conditions are present.

- A computer diagnosis trouble code (DTC) indicating the lack of EGR flow
- The failure of an exhaust emission test for excessive NOx
- Excessive engine spark knock (ping or detonation)

_____ 1. Check service information for the recommended procedures to follow when servicing the EGR system.

_____

_____ 2. What problem(s) exists? _____

_____ 3. Remove the EGR valve and inspect for clogged passages. Clean as needed.

Valve was clogged _____    Valve was OK _____

_____ 4. Start the engine. Exhaust should be heard and felt coming from the open passage where the EGR valve was located.

**CAUTION:** Be sure to wear eye protection. Particles of carbon can be forced out of the EGR passage with great force when the engine starts.

Exhaust flowed freely _____    Exhaust did not flow freely _____

_____ 5. To clean the passages of carbon, remove the plugs or EGR valve and insert a stiff wire into an electric drill and use it to ream out the passages.

_____ 6. Reinstall the EGR valve with a new gasket and check the engine for proper operation.

_____ 7. What is the necessary action? _____

_____

# 128

# EGR Electrical Sensors

**Meets NATEF Task:** (A8-E-5) Inspect and test electrical/electronic sensors, controls, and wiring of exhaust gas recirculation (EGR) systems; perform necessary action. (P-2)

Name _____ Date _____ Time on Task _____

Make/Model _____ Year _____ Evaluation:  4  3  2  1

_____ **1.** Check service information for the recommended tests and diagnostic procedure to follow to diagnose EGR system sensors and controls.

_____

_____

_____

_____

_____

_____ **2.** List the tools and equipment needed as specified by the vehicle manufacturer. Check all that apply.

_____ Scan tool

_____ Vacuum pump

_____ Digital multimeter (DMM)

_____ 5-gas exhaust analyzer

_____ Other (describe) _____

_____ **3.** Based on the test results, what is the necessary action?

_____

_____

# 129

# Ford EVP Voltage Check

**Meets NATEF Task:** (A8-E-5) Inspect and test electrical/electronic sensors, controls, and wiring of exhaust gas recirculation (EGR) systems; perform necessary action. (P-2)

Name _____  Date _____  Time on Task _____

Make/Model _____  Year _____  Evaluation:  4  3  2  1

The EGR valve position (EVP) sensor is used by the PCM to provide feedback as to the actual position of the EGR valve. If the actual position and the commanded position are different, a diagnostic trouble code could be set. An EVP signal that is out-of-range can also cause an incorrect fuel mixture to be supplied to the engine. Compare the voltage reading to the percentage of EGR valve opening.

- Check that the valve is able to be fully closed (could be stuck with carbon).

- If the EVP is too low, ignition timing will be retarded.

_____ **1.** Check service information for the exact specification for the vehicle being tested (typical specification).

| EGR Opening Percentage | Black Sensor Volts | Gray Sensor Volts |
|---|---|---|
| 0% | 0.90 | 0.35 |
| 10% | 1.25 | 0.75 |
| 20% | 1.65 | 1.10 |
| 30% | 1.95 | 1.45 |
| 40% | 2.30 | 1.80 |
| 50% | 2.65 | 2.15 |
| 60% | 3.00 | 2.50 |
| 70% | 3.35 | 2.85 |
| 80% | 3.70 | 3.20 |
| 90% | 4.05 | 3.55 |
| 100% | 4.40 | 3.90 |

_____ **2.** Does the voltage and the commanded position as determined by a scan tool agree?

Yes _____ No _____

_____ **3.** Based on the test results, what is the necessary action? _____

# 130

# PCV System Inspection

**Meets NATEF Task:** (A8-E-1) Diagnose oil leaks, emissions, and driveability concerns caused by the positive crankcase ventilation (PCV) system; determine necessary action. (P-2)

**Name** Zach Warren     **Date** _____     **Time on Task** _____

**Make/Model** _____     **Year** _____     **Evaluation:** 4   3   2   1

✓ **1.** Check service information for the recommended steps to follow when testing or servicing the positive crankcase ventilation (PCV) system.

_____

_____

✓ **2.** Check service information and describe the location of the following:

PCV valve _under intake_____

Crankcase vent filter _N/A_____

Fixed orifice (if equipped) _____

_Secondary Air_
Other (describe) _Near ignition coil_

✓ **3.** What is specified replacement interval for the PCV valve?

_____

✓ **4.** Remove and clear the PCV valve (if equipped) and note the condition.

   ✓ Like new      ____ Very dirty

   ____ Slightly dirty      ____ Valve clogged or stuck

   ____ Other (describe) _____

✓ **5.** Based on the test and inspection and on the recommendation of the vehicle manufacturer, what is the necessary action?

_____

# 131

# PCV System Diagnosis

**Meets NATEF Task:** (A8-E-2) Inspect, test and service positive crankcase ventilation (PCV) filter/breather cap, valve, tubes, orifices, and hoses; perform necessary action. (P-2)

Name _Zach, Warren_     Date _____     Time on Task _____

Make/Model _____     Year _____     Evaluation: 4  3  2  1

✓ **1.** Check service information for the recommended procedures to follow when diagnosing the PCV system.

**TO INTAKE MANIFOLD**

**TO CRANKCASE**

_____

_____

✓ **2.** Start the engine and allow it to idle and remove the oil fill cap.

✓ **3.** Place a piece of paper or a 3" × 5" card over the filler. (The PCV system is functioning correctly if the paper is held down tight onto the filler by vacuum in the crankcase).

✓ **4.** Seal off the oil fill opening and measure the crankcase vacuum at the dipstick tube = _____ (should be about 0.5 in. Hg. or 7 in. or more of water if using a water manometer).

OK _✓_    NOT OK _____

✓ **5.** Based on the test results, what is the necessary action?

_nothing_ _____

_____

_____

# 132

# Secondary Air Injection Diagnosis

**Meets NATEF Task:** (A8-E-6) Diagnose emissions and driveability concerns caused by the secondary air injection and catalytic converter systems; determine necessary action. (P-2)

Name _Zach Warren_  Date _____  Time on Task _____

Make/Model _____  Year _____  Evaluation: 4 3 2 1

AIR means "air injection reaction." An AIR pump supplies additional air to the exhaust system to reduce carbon monoxide (CO) and unburned gasoline (hydrocarbons or HC) exhaust emissions. Most AIR pump systems supply air to the exhaust manifold (exhaust ports) until the engine reaches closed loop operation. As soon as the computer reaches closed loop, the air flow is directed to the catalytic converter to help the catalyst oxidize the HC and CO into harmless water ($H_2O$) and carbon dioxide ($CO_2$).

✓ 1. Check service information for the recommended test procedure and specifications for the secondary air injection system.

N/A

✓ 2. Locate the air pump.

✓ 3. Carefully inspect the condition of all of the hoses, check the valves and the metal lines for corrosion or damage.

✓ 4. Start the engine and feel the air pump lines to confirm the proper air flow.

**NOTE:** A defective one-way check valve at the exhaust manifold can allow hot exhaust gases to flow past the check valve and cause damage to the switching valves, hoses or air pump itself. These exhaust gases can cause poor engine operation and stalling if drawn into the air intake system.

✓ 5. Inspect the air pump drive belt for cracks and proper tension or electrical connections for an electric air pump.

✓ 6. Based on the inspection and test results, what is the necessary action?

N/A

# 133

# AIR Pump Component Inspection

**Meets NATEF Task:** (A8-E-7) Inspect and test mechanical components of secondary air injection systems; perform necessary action. (P-3)

**Name** Zach, Warren     **Date** _____     **Time on Task** _____

**Make/Model** _____     **Year** _____     **Evaluation:** 4   3   2   1

✓ 1. Check service information for the recommended procedures to follow when inspecting and testing the AIR pump components.

N/A _____

✓ 2. Carefully inspect the condition of all of the hoses, check the valves and the metal lines for corrosion or damage.

✓ 3. Start the engine and feel the air pump lines to confirm the proper air flow.

**NOTE:** A defective one-way check valve at the exhaust manifold can allow hot exhaust gases to flow past the check valve and cause damage to the switching valves, hoses or air pump itself. These exhaust gases can cause poor engine operation and stalling if drawn into the air intake system.

✓ 4. Inspect the air pump drive belt for cracks and proper tension.

✓ 5. Based on the inspection, what is the necessary action?

N/A _____

_____

_____

# 134

# AIR Pump Electrical Component Inspection

**Meets NATEF Task:** (A8-E-8) Inspect and test electrical/electronically-operated components and circuits of air injection systems; perform necessary action. (P-3)

**Name** _Zach, Warren_     **Date** _____     **Time on Task** _____

**Make/Model** _____     **Year** _____     **Evaluation:  4   3   2   1**

____   1. Check service information for the recommended procedures, tests, and specifications for inspecting and testing the electrical/electronic component of the secondary air injection system.

_____

_____

____   2. List the tools and equipment specified by the vehicle manufacturer to diagnose the electrical/electronic components of the secondary air injection system. Check all that apply.

     ____ Digital multimeter (DMM)

     ____ Scan tool

     ____ Exhaust gas analyzer

     ____ Other (describe)

     _____

     _____

     _____

____   3. Based on the inspection and tests, what is the necessary action?

_____

_____

# 135

We Support
NATEF

# Exhaust System Backpressure Test

**Meets NATEF Task:** (A8-D-9) Perform exhaust system back-pressure test; determine necessary action. (P-1)

Name _____    Date _____    Time on Task _____

Make/Model _____    Year _____    Evaluation: 4 3 2 1

A clogged or partially restricted exhaust greatly affects engine performance. Lack of power is a common symptom of a partially restricted exhaust system. In severe cases, the engine may start/stall due to exhaust system restriction.

_____ 1. Check service information for the specified maximum backpressure. _____

_____

_____ 2. Remove the oxygen sensor from the exhaust manifold and install tool to measure exhaust back pressure.

**NOTE:** This tool can be made from an 18 mm fitting and a vacuum hose nipple.

_____ 3. Connect a vacuum/pressure gauge to the exhaust back pressure tool. Start the engine and run at idle and observe exhaust back pressure.

   _____ psi back pressure (maximum allowable back pressure at idle is 1.25 psi.)

   OK _____        NOT OK _____

_____ 4. Operate the engine at a constant speed of 2500 RPM and observe the exhaust back pressure.

   _____ psi back pressure (Maximum allowable back pressure at 2500 RPM is 2.5 psi.)

   OK _____        NOT OK _____

_____ 5. Based on the results of the backpressure test, what is the necessary action?

_____

# 136

# Catalytic Converter Test

**Meets NATEF Task:** (A8-E-9) Inspect and test catalytic converter efficiency. (P-1)

---

Name _____ Date _____ Time on Task _____

Make/Model _____ Year _____ Evaluation: 4  3  2  1

_____ 1. Check service information for the recommended test to perform on the catalytic converter.

_____

_____

_____ 2. The recommended test(s) include the following. Check all that apply.

　　　_____ Check for loose substrate (rattle noise)

　　　_____ Check temperature differences

　　　_____ Use propane

　　　_____ Use an exhaust gas analyzer

　　　_____ Other (describe) _____

_____ 3. Which tests were performed and what were the results?

　　　a. _____ Result: _____

　　　b. _____ Result: _____

　　　c. _____ Result: _____

_____ 4. Based on the tests and inspection of the catalytic converter, what is the necessary action?

_____

_____

# 137

# Catalytic Converter Rattle Test

**Meets NATEF Task:** (A8-E-9) Inspect and test catalytic converter efficiency. (P-1)

**Name** _____ **Date** _____ **Time on Task** _____

**Make/Model** _____ **Year** _____ **Evaluation:** 4 3 2 1

_____ **1.** Safely hoist the vehicle.

_____ **2.** Using your fist or a small rubber mallet, lightly tap on the catalytic converter. If the

converter rattles, it is broken internally and requires replacement.

> **NOTE:** If the catalytic converter has broken substrate, the muffler may also require replacement.

_____ **3.** Based on the results of this test, what is the necessary action? _____

_____

# 138

# Catalytic Converter Performance Test

**Meets NATEF Task:** (A8-E-9) Inspect and test catalytic converter efficiency. (P-1)

Name _____  Date _____  Time on Task _____

Make/Model _____  Year _____  Evaluation: 4  3  2  1

### (Temperature Difference)

A catalytic converter uses a catalyst to start a chemical reaction, but does not enter into the chemical reaction. Because a chemical reaction causes heat, the temperature of the catalytic converter should be at least 10% hotter at the outlet as compared to the temperature of the inlet.

_____ 1. Start the engine and run at a fast idle (2500 RPM) for at least 2 minutes to fully warm up the oxygen sensor, the engine coolant and catalytic converter.

_____ 2. Using a pyrometer (infrared or contact type), measure the front (inlet) and outlet of the catalytic converter.

        Inlet temperature   = _____ °

        Outlet temperature = _____ °

        Difference         = _____ °

_____ 3. Results: If the outlet temperature is 50°F (10°C) (or 10%) higher than the inlet temperature, the catalytic converter is functioning correctly. **OK** ___ **NOT OK** ___

> **NOTE:** Some engines are operating so cleanly that the catalytic converter has limited emissions to convert and therefore, the temperature of the converter may not show an increase in temperature. To check if the catalytic converter is functioning on a vehicle with very low exhaust emissions, simply use a vacuum hose connected to a spark plug wire and temporarily ground out one cylinder by using a tester light or jumper wire attached to ground. Measure the inlet and outlet temperatures of the converter while one cylinder is grounded out. To avoid damage to the catalytic converter, do not ground out a cylinder for longer than 10 seconds.

_____ 4. Based on the test results, what is the necessary action? _____

_____

# 139

# Ignition System Identification

**Meets NATEF Task:** (A8-A-3) Research applicable vehicle and service information, such as engine management system operation, vehicle service history, service precautions, and TSBs. (P-1)

---

**Name** _____  **Date** _____  **Time on Task** _____

**Make/Model** _____  **Year** _____  **Evaluation:** 4  3  2  1

_____ 1. Check service information and determine what type of ignition system is used on this vehicle?

_____ Distributor ignition (DI)
_____ Waste-spark (EI)
_____ Coil-on-plug
_____ Other (describe)
_____
_____

_____ 2. Check service information and determine what type of primary circuit switching device is used on this system.

_____ Pickup coil (pulse generator)  Used on most distributor-type ignition systems.
_____ Hall-effect sensor
_____ Magnetic sensor
_____ Optical sensor
_____ Other (describe) _____

_____ 3. What color wires are used on the switching device?

_____, _____, _____, _____

_____ 4. Using service information, determine where the primary ignition switching device signal goes:

_____ Ignition control module (ICM)
_____ Computer (PCM)
_____ Other (describe) _____

# 140

# Electronic Ignition Diagnosis

**Meets NATEF Task:** (A8-C-1) Diagnose electronic ignition-related problems; determine necessary action. (P-1)

---

Name _____     Date _____     Time on Task _____

Make/Model _____     Year _____     Evaluation:  4  3  2  1

_____  **1.** Check service information for the specified diagnostic procedures to follow when troubleshooting the ignition system.

_____

_____

_____

_____  **2.** Most test procedures specify that the spark be tested using a spark tester. Use a spark tester and determine that a spark does occur at each cylinder.

       Cylinder #1 _____   **OK** ____  **NOT OK** ____  (describe) _____

       Cylinder #2 _____   **OK** ____  **NOT OK** ____  (describe) _____

       Cylinder #3 _____   **OK** ____  **NOT OK** ____  (describe) _____

       Cylinder #4 _____   **OK** ____  **NOT OK** ____  (describe) _____

       Cylinder #5 _____   **OK** ____  **NOT OK** ____  (describe) _____

       Cylinder #6 _____   **OK** ____  **NOT OK** ____  (describe) _____

       Cylinder #7 _____   **OK** ____  **NOT OK** ____  (describe) _____

       Cylinder #8 _____   **OK** ____  **NOT OK** ____  (describe) _____

_____  **3.** Based on the test results, what is the necessary action?

_____

_____

**TESTER**

# 141

# Ignition Scope Analysis

**Meets NATEF Task:** (A8-C-2) Inspect and test ignition primary and secondary circuit wiring and solid state components; test ignition coil(s); perform necessary action. (P-1)

Name _____  Date _____  Time on Task _____

Make/Model _____  Year _____  Evaluation:  4  3  2  1

_____ 1. Check service information regarding the specified method for attaching and using a secondary circuit oscilloscope.

_____

_____

_____ 2. Type of ignition:

_____ Distributor
_____ Waste spark
_____ Coil-on-plug

_____ 3. Connect the ignition scope to the system as per the scope manufacturer's instructions.

_____ 4. Brand of scope used: _____

_____ 5. Describe the hookup procedure. _____

_____ 6. Start the engine and observe the secondary ignition waveform.

| | **Firing Voltage (KV)**<br>(voltage should be 5-15 KV) | **Spark Line Length (ms)**<br>(length should be 1-2 ms) |
|---|---|---|
| **Cylinder #1** | _____ | _____ |
| **Cylinder #2** | _____ | _____ |
| **Cylinder #3** | _____ | _____ |
| **Cylinder #4** | _____ | _____ |
| **Cylinder #5** | _____ | _____ |
| **Cylinder #6** | _____ | _____ |
| **Cylinder #7** | _____ | _____ |
| **Cylinder #8** | _____ | _____ |

_____ 7. Based on the test results, what is the necessary action? _____

# 142

# Ignition Inspection and Testing

**Meets NATEF Task:** (A8-C-2) Inspect and test ignition primary and secondary circuit wiring and solid state components; test ignition coil(s); perform necessary action. (P-1)

Name _____ Date _____ Time on Task _____

Make/Model _____ Year _____ Evaluation: 4 3 2 1

_____ 1. Check service information for the specifications and testing procedures for the secondary ignition wiring.

_____

_____ 2. Carefully check the spark plug wire for damage or burned areas that could indicate a break in the insulation.

         OK _____     NOT OK _____

_____ 3. Set the digital multimeter to read ohms (Ω).

_____ 4. List the length in feet and the resistance values in ohms for each spark plug wire according to the cylinder number:

         **Length (feet)**     **Ohms**

     1. _____    _____
     2. _____    _____
     3. _____    _____
     4. _____    _____
     5. _____    _____
     6. _____    _____
     7. _____    _____
     8. _____    _____

Coil wire: (if equipped)

     _____    _____

_____ 5. Results - Original equipment radio suppression wires should test 10,000 ohms (10KΩ) or *less* per foot of length.

         OK _____     NOT OK _____

_____ 6. Based on the inspection and test(s), what is the necessary action? _____

_____

# 143

# Spark Plugs Inspection

**Meets NATEF Task:** (A8-C-2) Inspect and test ignition primary and secondary circuit wiring and solid state components; test ignition coil(s); perform necessary action. (P-1)

---

**Name** _____  **Date** _____  **Time on Task** _____

**Make/Model** _____  **Year** _____  **Evaluation:  4   3   2   1**

_____ **1.** Check service information and determine the correct plug code and gap for your vehicle using a spark plug application guide.

  Engine:  # Cylinders_____   VIN# _____

  Brand _____   Code # _____   Gap _____

_____ **2.** Remove and label all the spark plug wires.

_____ **3.** Determine the condition and gap of all spark plugs:

| | **Condition** | **Gap** |
|---|---|---|
| 1. | _____ | _____ |
| 2. | _____ | _____ |
| 3. | _____ | _____ |
| 4. | _____ | _____ |
| 5. | _____ | _____ |
| 6. | _____ | _____ |
| 7. | _____ | _____ |
| 8. | _____ | _____ |

_____ **4.** Reinstall the spark plug (start by hand).

_____ **5.** Use a torque wrench and torque the spark plugs to the proper torque.

  Specified torque = _____

_____ **6.** Start the engine.  Check for possible rough running caused by crossed or loose spark plug wires.

  **OK** _____      **NOT OK** _____

_____ **7.** Based on the inspection of the spark plugs, what is the necessary action? _____

_____

# 144

# Ignition Coil Testing

**Meets NATEF Task:** (A8-C-2) Inspect and test ignition primary and secondary circuit wiring and solid state components; test ignition coil(s); perform necessary action. (P-1)

Name _____ Date _____ Time on Task _____

Make/Model _____ Year _____ Evaluation: 4 3 2 1

_____ **1.** Check service information for the specified ignition coil testing procedure.

_____

_____ **2.** Visually inspect the coil(s) for carbon track and other faults. **OK ___ NOT OK ___**

_____ **3.** Check the primary winding resistance.

Specification: _____

Actual: _____

**OK ____ NOT OK ____**

_____ **4.** Check the secondary winding resistance.

Specification: _____

Actual: _____

**OK ____ NOT OK ____**

_____ **5.** Perform resistance checks for short-to-ground.

**OK ____ NOT OK ____**

_____ **6.** Based on the inspection and tests, what is the necessary action? _____

_____

# 145

# Primary Ignition Inspection and Testing

**Meets NATEF Task:** (A8-C-3 and A8-C-4) Inspect, test, and/or replace ignition control module, powertrain/engine control module; reprogram as necessary. (P-2)

Name _____ Date _____ Time on Task _____

Make/Model _____ Year _____ Evaluation: 4 3 2 1

_____ 1. Check service information and determine what type of ignition system is used on this vehicle?

       _____ Distributor ignition (DI)
       _____ Waste-spark (EI)
       _____ Coil-on-plug
       _____ Other (describe) _____

_____ 2. Check service information and determine what type of primary circuit switching device is used on this system.

       _____ Pickup coil (pulse generator) Used on most distributor-type ignition systems.
       _____ Hall-effect sensor
       _____ Magnetic sensor
       _____ Optical sensor
       _____ Other (describe) _____

_____ 3. Check service information and determine what color wires are used on the switching device?

       _____, _____, _____, _____

_____ 4. The primary ignition switching device signal goes to the:

       _____ Ignition control module (ICM)
       _____ Computer (PCM)
       _____ Other (describe) _____

_____ 5. Using the service information, what are the steps to diagnosis a no-spark condition?

       _____
       _____
       _____

_____ 6. Could a fault in the primary ignition sensor cause a no-spark condition?

       Yes _____ No _____

_____ 7. Based on inspection and tests, what is the necessary action? _____

# 146

# ENGINE PERFORMANCE DIAGNOSIS

**Meets NATEF Task:** (A8-A-2) Identify and interpret engine performance concern; determine necessary action. (P-1)

Name _____  Date _____  Time on Task _____

Make/Model _____  Year _____  Evaluation: 4  3  2  1

| (PLEASE CIRCLE ALL THAT APPLY IN ALL CATEGORIES) | |
|---|---|
| **Describe Problem:** | |
| **When Did the Problem First Occur?** | • Just Started  • Last Week  • Last Month  • Other _____ |
| **List Previous Repairs in the Last 6 Months:** | |
| **Starting Problems** | • Will Not Crank  • Cranks, But Will Not Start  • Starts, But Takes A Long Time |
| **Engine Quits or Stalls** | • Right After Starting  • When Put Into Gear  • During Steady Speed Driving  • Right After Vehicle Comes To A Stop  • While Idling  • During Acceleration  • When Parking |
| **Poor Idling Conditions** | • Is Too Slow At All Times  • Is Too Fast  • Intermittently Too Fast or Too Slow  • Is Rough or Uneven  • Fluctuates Up and Down |
| **Poor Running Conditions** | • Runs Rough  • Lacks Power  • Bucks and Jerks  • Poor Fuel Economy  • Hesitates or Stumbles On Acceleration  • Backfires  • Misfires or Cuts Out  • Engine Knocks, Pings, Rattles  • Surges  • Dieseling or Run-On |
| **Auto. Transmission Problems** | • Improper Shifting (early/late)  • Changes Gear Incorrectly  • Vehicle Does Not Move When In Gear  • Jerks or Bucks |
| **Usually Occurs** | • Morning  • Afternoon  • Anytime |
| **Engine Temperature** | • Cold  • Warm  • Hot |
| **Driving Conditions During Occurrence** | • Short-Less Than 2 Miles  • 2-10 Miles  • Long-More Than 10 Miles  • Stop and Go  • While Turning  • While Braking  • At Gear Engagement  • With A/C Operating  • With Headlights On  • During Acceleration  • During Deceleration  • Mostly Downhill  • Mostly Uphill  • Mostly Level  • Mostly curvy  • Rough Road |
| **Driving Habits** | • Mostly City Driving  • Highway  • Park Vehicle Inside  • Park Vehicle Outside  **Drive Per Day:**  • Less Than 10 Miles  • 10-50  • More Than 50 |
| **Gasoline Used** | **Fuel Octane:**  • 87  • 89  • 91  • More Than 91  **Brand:** _____ |
| **Temperature When Problem Occurs** | • 32-55° F  • Below Freezing (32° F)  • Above 55° F |
| **Check Engine Light/ Dash Warning Light** | • Light on Sometimes  • Light on Always  • Light Never On |
| **Smells** | • "Hot"  • Gasoline  • Oil Burning  • Electrical |
| **Noises** | • Rattle  • Knock  • Squeak  • Other |

# 147

# Retrieving OBD II Diagnostic Trouble Codes

**Meets NATEF Task:** (A8-B-1) Retrieve and record diagnostic trouble codes, OBD monitor status, and freeze frame data; clear codes when applicable. (P-1)

Name _____ Date _____ Time on Task _____

Make/Model _____ Year _____ Evaluation: 4 3 2 1

A scan tool is required to retrieve diagnostic trouble codes from an OBD II vehicle. Every OBD II scan tool will be able to read all generic **Society of Automotive Engineers (SAE)** DTCs from any vehicle.

_____ 1. Retrieve the DTCs using a scan tool.

(Specify which scan tool was used = _____.)

_____ _____ _____ _____ _____

_____ 2. If no DTCs are displayed, set a DTC by disconnecting a sensor such as the throttle position (TP) sensor and then starting and running the engine.

_____ 3. Did the scan tool display both a generic OBD II (Poxxx) code *and* a manufacturer's specific DTC (P1xxx) code?

Yes _____ No _____

_____ 4. Clear the stored DTCs using the scan tool.

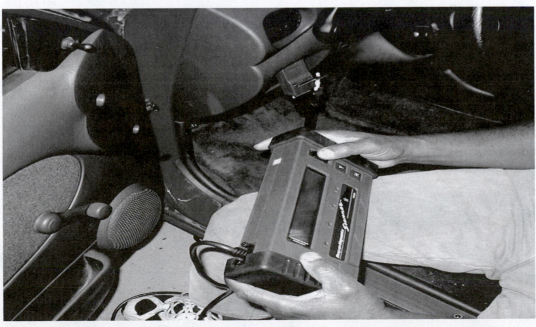

# Set Opposite Code

**Meets NATEF Task:** (A8-B-2) Diagnose the causes of emissions or driveability concerns resulting from malfunctions in the computerized engine control system with stored diagnostic trouble codes. (P-1)

Name _____ Date _____ Time on Task _____

Make/Model _____ Year _____ Evaluation: 4 3 2 1

If a diagnostic trouble code is set, a commonly used method of diagnosis is to attempt to set the opposite code after clearing the original code. For example, if a throttle position (TP) code is set, clear the DTC and attempt to set a DTC for the opposite condition.

- If a signal high DTC is set, clear the code and turn the ignition switch on (engine off), unplug the sensor and a signal low DTC should be set.

- If a signal low DTC is set, unplug the sensor connector and using a jumper wire, connect the 5-volt reference to the signal terminal in the connector (not at the sensor). Turn the ignition switch on (engine off) and the opposite DTC should set.

_____ 1. Set a DTC for TP or MAP sensor.

      a. Which sensor was used? _____
      b. What code set? _____
      c. Meaning of code set? _____

_____ 2. Clear the DTC.

_____ 3. Disconnect the sensor wiring and use a jumper wire to set the opposite code.

      a. What code was set? _____
      b. **OK** _____ **NOT OK** _____

**Results:**

If the opposite code *does* set, the cause of the original DTC is the result of a fault in the sensor (component) itself.

If the opposite DTC *does not* set, the problem is likely due to a wiring fault.

**NOTE:** Always consult a factory service manual for the factors that must be met for a DTC to be set. Be sure that all factors are present when attempting to set the opposite code.

# Freeze Frame and MIL Activity

**Meets NATEF Task:** (A8-B-2) Diagnose the causes of emissions or driveability concerns resulting from malfunctions in the computerized engine control system with stored DTCs. (P-1)

Name _____  Date _____  Time on Task _____

Make/Model _____  Year _____  Evaluation: 4  3  2  1

The purpose of this activity is to allow the service technician apply the use of freeze frames in the diagnosis of OBD II faults.

_____ 1. Connect a scan tool with the key on, engine off (KOEO), and disconnect the electrical connection from the throttle position (TP) sensor. Wait 3 seconds.

_____ 2. A TP sensor TP fault diagnostic trouble code (DTC) should have been set.

        ____ Yes (DTC was set)      ____ No (no DTC was set) Turn the ignition off and back on.  Did the DTC set?
                                                  ____ Yes ____ No

_____ 3. Using a scan tool, view the freeze frame created when the DTC was set.

        ____ OK (freeze frame was set) ____ No (freeze frame was not set)

_____ 4. Is the malfunction indicator lamp (MIL or check engine) on?  ____ Yes ____ No

_____ 5. Check service information and list the reason(s) that could cause the MIL to be on in the event of a disconnected TP sensor.

    _____

    _____

_____ 6. Check service information and determine what needs to occur to turn off the MIL.

    _____

    _____

DLC CONNECTOR

SCAN TOOL CONNECTED TO THE DLC

| 1 | 2 | 3 | 4 | 5 | 6 | 7 | 8 |

| 9 | 10 | 11 | 12 | 13 | 14 | 15 | 16 |

16 PIN OBD II DATA LINK CONNECTOR (DLC)

# 150

We Support
NATEF

# Misfire Monitor Activity

**Meets NATEF Task:** (A8-B-3) Diagnose emissions or driveability concerns without stored diagnostic trouble codes; determine necessary action. (P-1)

Name _____ Date _____ Time on Task _____

Make/Model _____ Year _____ Evaluation: 4  3  2  1

_____ 1. Check service information for the details regarding how the misfire monitor reacts to a misfire and under what engine operating conditions.

> HO2S Data
> Misfire Data
> EVAP Data

_____

_____

_____ 2. Connect a scan tool to the data link connector (DLC) and create a misfire. (Use a spark tester connected to one removed spark plug wire to create an ignition misfire without doing any harm to the vehicle.)

_____ 3. Observe the misfire monitor on the scan tool and record. _____

_____

_____ 4. Rapidly depress the accelerator pedal to wide-open throttle (WOT) a few times. Did the misfire monitor change?

____ Yes ____ No Explain: _____

_____

_____ 5. Turn the ignition key off, and then back on. Did a misfire diagnostic trouble code (DTC) set?

____ Yes ____ No

_____ 6. Check freeze frame information on the scan tool. Was freeze frame stored?

____ Yes ____ No Why? _____

_____ 7. Based on this activity, what action is necessary? _____

# 151

# Service Information Diagnosis

**Meets NATEF Task:** (A8-B-6) Access and use service information to perform step-by-step diagnosis. (P-1)

Name _____  Date _____  Time on Task _____

Make/Model _____  Year _____  Evaluation: 4  3  2  1

Check service information and determine the specified step-by-step diagnosis for the following problems.

_____ **1.** Rough/unstable idle – no DTCs: _____

_____

_____

_____ **2.** Hesitation during acceleration – no DTCs: _____

_____

_____

_____ **3.** Engine noise when cold: _____

_____

_____

_____ **4.** P0300 (misfire DTC): _____

_____

_____

# 152

# Drive Trace Pre-Conditioning

**Meets NATEF Task:** (A8-B-7) Diagnose driveability and emissions problems resulting from malfunctions of interrelated systems, etc; determine necessary action. (P-3)

---

Name _____ Date _____ Time on Task _____

Make/Model _____ Year _____ Evaluation: 4 3 2 1

_____ **1.** Check service information for the specified drive trace pre-conditioning procedures for the following monitors:

      a. All monitors: _____

      _____

      _____

      b. Oxygen sensor heater monitor: _____

      _____

      c. Oxygen sensor monitor: _____

      _____

      d. Catalytic converter monitor: _____

      _____

      e. Evaporative emission control (EVAP) monitor: _____

      _____

      f. Exhaust gas recirculation (EGR) monitor:_____

      _____

```
              Powertrain


F0: Diagnostic Trouble Codes (DTC)
F1: Data Display
F2: Special Functions
F3: Snapshot
F4: I/M System Information
F5: ID Information
```

```
            I/M System Status

Emission Related DTC(s):
  Number of DTC(s)           3
  MIL Requested            YES

Test                    Completed
Catalyst                    No
EVAP                        No
HO2S/O2S                    No
HO2S Heater                 No
EGR                         No
```

# 153

We Support NATEF

# Scan Tool Active Test

**Meets NATEF Task:** (A8-B-8) Perform active tests of actuators using scan tool; determine necessary action. (P-1)

Name _____ Date _____ Time on Task _____

Make/Model _____ Year _____ Evaluation: 4 3 2 1

_____ 1. Check service information for the recommended procedure and designated scan tool to

use to perform actuator testing. _____

_____

_____ 2. The actuators can be controlled using a
scan tool include (check all that apply):

     _____ EGR

     _____ Idle air control (IAC)

     _____ Injectors (balance test)

     _____ Transmission shifting

     _____ Torque converter clutch apply

     _____ Other (describe) _____

```
                PC Solenoid

         Commanded State:  None

             PC Solenoid Data

PC Sol. Actual Current        0.00 amps
PC Sol. Ref. Current          0.00 amps
PC Solenoid Duty Cycle           0 %
Engine Speed                     0 RPM
Trans. Fluid Temp.              87 °F
                               1 / 8  -
PC Sol. Actual Current

 Quick    Decrease   Increase    More
Snapshot
```

_____ 3. Perform active tests of actuators using a scan tool.

| Unit Tested | Results |
|---|---|
| A. _____ | _____ |
| B. _____ | _____ |
| C. _____ | _____ |
| D. _____ | _____ |

_____ 4. Based on the results of the active tests, what is the necessary action? _____

_____

# 154

# I/M Monitors Status

**Meets NATEF Task:** (A8-B-9) Describe the importance of running all OBD II monitors for repair verification. (P-1)

---

Name _____  Date _____  Time on Task _____

Make/Model _____  Year _____  Evaluation: 4 3 2 1

_____ 1. Check service information for the specified procedures and test equipment needed to determine the status of the inspection and maintenance (I/M) monitors.

_____

_____

_____ 2. Connect a scan tool and check the status of the I/M monitors and list their status.

| Monitor | Status |
| --- | --- |
| _____ | _____ |
| _____ | _____ |
| _____ | _____ |
| _____ | _____ |
| _____ | _____ |

_____ 3. Check service information and determine under what condition the vehicle must be driven to have the monitors run.

_____

_____ 4. Based on the results, what is the necessary action? _____

_____

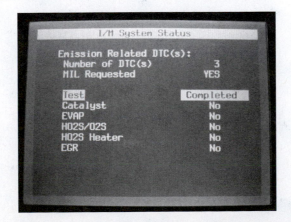

# 155

# Driveability and Emission Problem Diagnosis

**Meets NATEF Task:** (A8-B-9) Diagnose driveability and emission concerns due to related vehicle systems; determine necessary action. (P-3)

Name _____  Date _____  Time on Task _____

Make/Model _____  Year _____  Evaluation:  4  3  2  1

_____ **1.** Check service information for the procedure to follow when diagnosing driveability and/or emission concerns that may be related to other systems in the vehicle.

_____

_____

_____ **2.** List all non-OEM-installed accessories. _____

_____

_____ **3.** Disconnect or disable all non-factory accessories.

_____ **4.** Is the driveability- or emission-related fault affected by the aftermarket accessory?

_____

_____ **5.** Check the operation of all other vehicle systems and check if their operation affects the driveability or emission fault.

_____ Yes (which component or accessory) _____

_____ No

_____ **6.** Based on the testing, what is the necessary action? _____

_____

# 156

We Support
NATEF

# Hybrid Vehicle HV Circuit Disconnect

**Meets NATEF Task:** (A6-B-7) Identify high-voltage circuits of electric or hybrid electric vehicle and related safety precautions. (P-3)

Name _____ Date _____ Time on Task _____

Make/Model _____ Year _____ Evaluation: 4  3  2  1

_____ 1. Check service information for the location of the high-voltage disconnect (service plug) for the following hybrid electric vehicles:

       Toyota Prius _____

       _____

       Toyota Camry hybrid _____

       _____

       Honda Civic and Accord hybrid _____

       _____

       Ford/Mercury hybrid _____

       General Motors PHT hybrid _____

       General Motors two-mode hybrid _____

       Saturn hybrid _____

       Other (describe) _____

_____ 2. Check service information and list the safety precautions specified when de-powering the high-voltage circuits.

       _____

       _____

       _____

# 157

# Hybrid ICE Service Precautions

**Meets NATEF Task:** (A8-F-7)

Identify hybrid internal combustion engine service precautions. (P-3)

Name _____ Date _____ Time on Task _____

Make/Model _____ Year _____ Evaluation:  4  3  2  1

_____ **1.** Using service information, determine the internal combustion engine service

precautions: _____

_____

_____

_____ **2.** Place a check mark (√) next to each item that was included or found in the service

information?

_____ Be sure the ignition is off.

_____ Be certain that the "ready" light is out.

_____ Use caution around hot surfaces.

_____ Disable the high-voltage (HV) electrical system.

_____ Disconnect a fuse or relay.

_____ Remove a service plug.

_____ Disconnect the 12-volt auxiliary battery.

_____ Other (describe) _____

_____ **3.** Does the vehicle manufacturer specify that high-voltage linesman's gloves be used?

___ Yes ___ No   If yes, when?

_____

# 158

We Support
NATEF
ASE CERTIFIED

# Electric/Fuel Cell Vehicle Identification

**Meets NATEF Task:** (A6-B-8) Identify high-voltage circuits of electric vehicles and related safety precautions. (P-3)

Name _____ Date _____ Time on Task _____

Make/Model _____ Year _____ Evaluation: 4 3 2 1

_____ **1.** Search service information for information on electric vehicles.

| | Brand/Model | Type of Batteries | Voltage | Charging Method |
|---|---|---|---|---|
| A. | _____ | _____ | _____ | _____ |
| B. | _____ | _____ | _____ | _____ |
| C. | _____ | _____ | _____ | _____ |
| D. | _____ | _____ | _____ | _____ |
| E. | _____ | _____ | _____ | _____ |

_____ **2.** Check service information for related safety precautions.

_____

_____